"Mindfulness can often one more thing we hav unparalleled ability to g. ....ness and make it accessible, clear, and approachable. Catherine's style reflects respect for the depth of the topic, but in the tone of a dear friend with warmth, compassion, and humor. An outstanding companion for anyone seeking peace, ease, and clarity."

—**Steven D. Hickman, PsyD**, clinical psychologist, executive director of the Center for Mindful Self-Compassion, and founding director of the UC San Diego Center for Mindfulness

"In your hands, you hold a beautiful and nuanced guide to living in deep harmony with your true, wise, compassionate, perfectly imperfect, and ever-loveable self. Catherine Polan Orzech offers a fresh look at wisdom teachings, inviting us to look through a new lens at our lives, and see ourselves and others with deep compassion and forgiveness."

—**Doris Ferleger, PhD**, mindfulness-based psychologist, and award-winning poet and author

"*A Moment for Me* is a like a smorgasbord that you digest slowly in small, delicious pieces over the course of a full year. Catherine's inviting language has a sense of lightness and poetry to it that gently leads you to weekly practices that can have deep, transformative effects. Little by little, this book expands our sense of ourselves, and our ability to live from love and see that we are all connected in the web of life."

—**Martin Wikfalk**, founder and CEO of The Mindfulness App

"*A Moment for Me* is a true treasure, a shining light full of wise, heartful reflections and mindfulness practices that will nourish your body, mind, and spirit. May you savor the gifts of care, kindness, and compassion offered in this beautiful book."

—**Diane Reibel, PhD**, director of the Myrna Brind Center for Mindfulness at Thomas Jefferson University Hospital, coauthor of *Teaching Mindfulness*, and coeditor of *Resources for Teaching Mindfulness*

"These mindfulness rituals open us to the beauty, goodness, and potential for awakening that is available every day of our lives."

—**Tara Brach**, author of *Radical Acceptance* and *Radical Compassion*

"With clarity and heart, Catherine Orzech has offered a practical, accessible guide to mindfulness practice. Weaving poignant stories with experiential practice, she's created a beautiful road map that highlights the best of contemporary teachings. These are grounded, well-earned insights that will surely serve you in your practice."

—**David Treleaven, PhD**, author of *Trauma-Sensitive Mindfulness*

A Moment for Me

52 SIMPLE MINDFULNESS PRACTICES TO SLOW DOWN, RELIEVE STRESS & NOURISH THE SPIRIT

CATHERINE POLAN ORZECH

REVEAL PRESS

Publisher's Note

This publication is designed tow provide accurate and authoritative information in regard to the subject matter covered. It is sold with the understanding that the publisher is not engaged in rendering psychological, financial, legal, or other professional services.

Distributed in Canada by Raincoast Books

Copyright © 2020 by Catherine Polan Orzech
          Reveal Press
          An imprint of New Harbinger Publications, Inc.
          5674 Shattuck Avenue
          Oakland, CA 94609
          www.newharbinger.com

Cover design by Amy Shoup; Acquired by Ryan Buresh;
Text design by Michele Waters-Kermes and Amy Shoup

Printed in the China

Library of Congress Cataloging-in-Publication Data on file

Printed in the United States of America

21 20 19

10 9 8 7 6 5 4 3 2 1   First Printing

For Michelle Kalman—my constant friend and companion in exploring the inner workings of the heart.

Contents

DECEMBER: DARKNESS AND LIGHT

Introduction

Many years ago, I underwent months of rehabilitative vision therapy after a concussion. As part of the treatment, the doctors had me wear all different types of lenses that distorted and changed my usual way of seeing in order to activate different parts of my brain.

Not surprisingly, things looked different. But more than that, I found that simply changing the lenses through which I looked at the world altered in some profound way my entire experience of myself and the world around me.

It is the same with developing mindfulness. If you wear a lens of striving or fixing, you will create a certain result. If you meet your life as it arises with a lens of affectionate interest, that will have a different outcome. The very attitudes we bring to mindfulness change our perception of reality and, therefore, our experience of life.

Depending on which lenses of attitude and perception we use to encounter our lives, our experience of reality can be transformed. Mindfulness enables us to study the human heart and mind and to understand the conditions that either give rise to stress and suffering or to the causes that give rise to their release. What we find when we look inward can lead to a deeper understanding of ourselves and a greater ability to live from love. But this requires a kind of curious, investigative attention. If you were a biologist and wanted to learn about the nature of some animal, you'd let it just do its thing in its natural habitat while you carefully observed it. The data that is collected through this study reveals the animal's true nature. We use mindfulness to study the mind and heart to allow us to know their nature and to be liberated from living in a trance—that unconscious state of being carried along by our own mental stories and habitual reactions to life. Mindfulness can provide the clear lens through which we can see the causes of our suffering.

This book does not aim to teach you the specifics of how to meditate. It is a collection of reflections and invitations, along with practices that can help us investigate and develop small and subtle shifts in our attitudes and perceptions in relation to our lives. But these small shifts can have a huge impact on our clear seeing and thus the quality of our lives.

The reflections and practices offered in this book are a deep dive into the heart and soul of what mindfulness is really about. Instead of delving into the popular notions of self-improvement, better concentration, and increased productivity, they aim to cultivate self-knowledge, wisdom, and compassion.

This book is for you if you have never meditated or thought about practicing mindfulness. It's also for you if you have been dabbling in mindfulness but haven't yet developed a focus on the attitudes of mind and heart that will enrich your learning. And if you have been meditating for years, you can use it to reacquaint yourself with what supports your practice and as a springboard for deepening inquiry into specific areas. The chapters that follow invite all of you into a rich friendship with your own heart and your own life.

A Moment for Me is laid out in fifty-two chapters with monthly themes. Each chapter contains a core concept, along with a reflection on that concept, and suggestions for practicing and incorporating that concept as a ritual into your life. The reflection and practice sections are marked by icons:

You can use this book in a variety of ways. Choose the one that works best for you:

- Develop a weekly ritual of following the chapter that corresponds to the week in the calendar year.

- Get a group of friends together and support each other each week, using the book as a discussion platform.

- Look through the themes and focus on whatever calls to you right now.

- Read the whole book and then go back to what stood out to you and specifically focus on that theme for a while.

- Pick up the book and randomly open it to whatever page asks to be read.

The approaches are endless and entirely up to you.

Although I am a teacher and therapist, I am still very much a student of my own teachers. Their wisdom is alive in me, and I have attempted to draw on it in writing this book. I hope that I have represented what I have learned from them faithfully. And if in any way I have not, I ask forgiveness.

Some of the teachers that I want to honor and acknowledge are Tara Brach, Pema Chödrön, and Mark Nunberg, who along with many other dharma teachers have offered some of the richest spiritual food that has nourished me throughout my life. If you are familiar with their teachings, you will likely hear echoes of their wisdom in this book. You'll also hear echoes of Jon Kabat-Zinn and the brilliance of mindfulness-based stress reduction, of Chris Germer and Kristin Neff's Mindful Self-Compassion program, and of the therapists behind the extremely beneficial mindfulness-based cognitive therapy protocol, among others. I draw on my years of learning from these programs while sitting in the role of teacher and from the hundreds of participants whom I've been honored to have in my classes.

As you enter into this book, taking these moments to pause, reflect on, and practice these offerings, may the qualities of affectionate curiosity, acceptance, patience, and love permeate your heart, mind, and body. May you also discover all the ways in which you already possess the essential ingredients for a life of joy and ease.

JANUARY

NEW BEGINNINGS

RITUAL

1

Intention and Attention

Almost every class on mindfulness begins with this question: *What brings you here?* What do we need to begin anything—an email, a new book, that long-overdue work assignment we've been avoiding?

We start any endeavor with an intention—a sense of resolve, a determination to act in a certain way, or the object of a prayer or devotion. In medicine, "intention" means a manner of healing.

Finding our intention is like finding a secret map from our heart. With that map, we can go on an adventure and explore our heart and mind—full of wonder, hopeful anticipation, and delight in the mysterious unfolding.

When we lose our way, our intention reorients us. Then, what we pay *attention* to can continually realign us with our intention and allow us to discover things that may otherwise remain hidden.

Intentions take faith. When we start out with the intention to walk, we begin each step—without consciously realizing it—by falling. We lift one foot off the floor, swing it forward, then shift our weight and "fall" onto it. Every step is a leap of faith. Will the ground be solid? Will our balance stabilize us? Will we have enough momentum to move forward?

Attention and intention are the ingredients for the adventure of living. When we align our conscious intentions with our actions, a natural flowering occurs, and eventually we will see the fruits of our intentions.

What Is Your Intention?

What is your intention as you read this book? If you're not sure, listen deeply to your heart and follow your curiosity.

Become aware of all that currently "holds you." How does it feel to be supported—by the floor, by your chair, by whatever solid surface is there for you? Allow your attention to expand, and feel your body. Let your awareness be permeated by friendly curiosity, an attentiveness that is accepting and allowing. Can you feel the flow of your breath? Can you feel the faithfulness of the breath and how in this moment it nourishes you?

Now imagine a well of very deep water, and allow the well in your imagination and the felt sense of your body to become one. Let yourself become the well.

Now ask yourself, *What is my intention for reading this book? What do I long for? What do I hope to gain or create?* Allow these questions to be like pebbles that hit the water of your "well," and watch as an answer "splashes up."

Allow whatever arises in your heart and mind just to be. Quietly sit with this intention and see how it feels.

 ## Be Guided by Your Intention

Use the guidance from the reflection to assist you in opening your mind and heart to "hear" your intention.

- As you listen, let your intention become a tangible phrase such as "May I deepen my connection to my heart and the wisdom the present moment contains."

- Start your day by taking a mindful pause even before you get out of bed and then repeat your intention.

- Write your intention on sticky notes and put the notes up in places where you will see them and be reminded of your intention.

- At the end of the day, take another mindful pause and check back in with your intention. Pay attention and see how it showed up for you and flowered throughout the day. This is not to "test yourself" or keep score but to actively practice self-kindness and support.

RITUAL

2

Releasing Striving,
Abiding in Wholeness

For most of my life, I was either outwardly or inwardly asking, "Am I doing it right?" I struggled when people told me to trust myself or my experience. I wanted *outside* proof that what I'd done was acceptable and pleasing to others. I can't say when this need for external validation began, but I know my fourth-grade teacher wrote about her concerns for my lack of self-confidence. Later, as a professional ballet dancer, that question followed me through the mirrors in the studio or the eyes of a choreographer or director. I didn't believe I could ever get away from it.

Even as an early student of meditation, I brought this same attitude to my practice. I would ask my teachers, "Am I doing it right?" And the teachers would say, "What do you think is supposed to be happening?" "What do you mean by '*right*'?" They encouraged me to get intimate with my own experience and study my own mind and heart for the answers. Eventually, something in me began to relax around the chronic striving for validation. I began to see it as striving—just another conditioned human tendency. I grew to know what striving felt like in my body and to recognize the thoughts that drove it—the whisperings of fear about whether I was "okay" just as I was.

The reality is, I am okay—and you are too.

All You Need Is Here

How would you experience this moment if you knew that all you really needed for *completeness* was already inside you? We often focus on what we perceive as not working. Even if there are parts of you are that are sick or struggling, that's not all of who you are. At this very moment, you have much more that is right with you than wrong. That's not just a pithy saying, it's true!

We don't have to stretch our minds too far to know it is true. We just need to shift our focus. Take the reality that right now, approximately thirty-seven trillion cells in your body are working for your benefit! You are alive right now because of the incredible workings of myriad systems. So, what are we really striving for? What do we mean when we wonder, *Am I okay?*

All of your past is now a memory and all of your future is but a dream. There is only the vibrant aliveness of this present moment. When you really feel this, something inside will begin to ease. You will feel the brilliance of your own symphony self, and you'll know you are back home.

Opening to Your Wholeness

Try this practice at least once per day this week.

- Take a moment to lie down and stretch yourself out on some cushioning on the floor.

- Let yourself be fully held by the solidity of the floor and soften any extra places of holding and tension within your body.

- Now imagine those thirty-seven trillion cells at work within your body as little orbs of light illuminating and animating your being.

- Feel the whole and vibratory aliveness of your being. Offer some words of acknowledgment and appreciation for all that these cells are doing for you right now.

- Now place one hand on your heart and another on your belly, feel the breath moving through you, and say to yourself, *In this moment, I aspire to abide at the center of my being.*

- Really rest here and soak in this feeling of wholeness, aliveness, and completeness with nothing to strive for.

Take time each day to revel in the reality of your own wholeness.

RITUAL

3

Mind the Gap

"Mind the gap" is the recorded announcement that rings out in every London train station. It's a warning to pay attention to the space between the station platform and the train car. Those spaces can be tricky, even treacherous, if we're not paying attention.

Our own minds are like train stations. Trains of thought zoom in from the past full of memories we rehash. They zoom away to the future to plan and worry. The train station of the mind can get extremely busy! And through it all, the announcement is there: "Mind the gap."

And there is a gap, a small space that exists between thoughts. What would happen if we really "minded" it? If we really paid attention to which train of thought we were getting on and whether it was where we really wanted to go?

Imagine sleepwalking and getting on a random train. You'd wake up later confused and terrified, having ridden so far and having no clue how you got there. This happens all the time in our own minds. Thoughts come in while we're not paying attention and sweep us off into some story. We're minding our own business, and then some thought from the past comes to mind; before we know it, we are in full-blown anger or panic. We completely miss the lives we're actually living—and we end up in a mental and emotional state that feels dangerous.

Mind the gap.

We Can Always Begin Again

So, what do we do when we find ourselves carried off?

Mindfulness teaches us that every moment is a new beginning. Within every moment is a way to "mind" the gap. Noticing the pause and really being in it allows us to see where we are and what "train" we are getting on or off. If it's one we want to stay on, no problem. If it's one that is not leading us in any useful direction, we can choose to redirect.

When we rest in the breath, something in us settles down. We realize that the majority of our moments are made up of the everyday activities of living: chewing gum, drinking tea, working at a computer, talking with a friend, walking the dog. We're not actually in the terrifying story our mind may be telling us. We can get off that train and savor the life we're presently in.

The gap that exists in between thoughts is a space of pure being and wholeness where nothing is lacking. When we intentionally cultivate this present-moment awareness, we afford ourselves endless opportunities to "begin again."

Dwelling in the Gap

This week, make a commitment to cultivate the presence to dwell in the gap.

- Take a mindful pause and breathe, noticing the space or gap between thoughts.

- Take stock of what is actually happening in the present moment.

- Look around you and start to name what you see—the colors, shapes—and what you actually hear, smell, and even taste. Use your senses to just be as and where you are.

- Check out which "train of thought" is traveling through the station of your mind and choose whether you want to continue along it or get off and redirect.

RITUAL

4

Creating a Compass

Imagine you are at your own funeral and you are listening to somebody share a eulogy for you. What do you want to have been known for? How do you want to be remembered?

Or ask these questions: What you are living for? What are your *core values*—the values that, like a compass, guide you and make your life meaningful?

Our values guide us either consciously or unconsciously. When they are unconscious, they nag at our hearts with a feeling of emptiness or longing. Sometimes we try to ignore those feelings, blame our circumstances, or distract ourselves rather than looking inside to see what unmet need is calling for our attention.

When we are conscious of our core values, they can serve as beacons of light directing our choices and path. Like a lighthouse standing tall, guiding a ship through fog and waves, values help us navigate our course.

Our values are at the foundation of our needs. So often, even the word "need" brings up fear and judgment because so many of us fear being "needy." But what we're talking about here are the basic universal human needs of safety, love, and belonging. These needs motivate all our actions and reactions to life's circumstances. When you come to understand your core values, it's easier to live by them—to act in ways that are in alignment with your own heart.

What Do You Really Value?

This reflection is inspired by an exercise taught in the Mindful Self-Compassion program.

How do I tell the difference between what I really value and something that is just a societal expectation? If the value energizes you, it is likely a core value; if it doesn't and it feels more like a "should," then you've likely bumped into a societal expectation.

Here's a very small example of some universal core values. Read over this list and as you say each word to yourself, pay attention to what images, associations, and emotions come up for you. Does your body soften or tighten around a particular word? Does a particular value energize you, or does it feel more oppressive?

- autonomy
- beauty
- collaboration
- connection with nature
- honesty

- love

- loyalty

- productivity

- relationships

- success

These are just a few, but there are hundreds.

Asking ourselves *What do I value?* and *What is important to me?* helps us clarify what is really happening in our hearts. Only with a clear, mindful appraisal of what's happening, without judging the situation or ourselves, can we make new movements toward reconnecting with our values and getting our needs met.

 ## Keeping the End in Mind

Our values guide us to live our lives in the ways that are most meaningful to us. To live our lives fully, it is important to be mindful of our values each day.

- Take a mindful pause and think about the values that resonated with you from the Reflection. Write them down and see how they feel.

- Now write your own eulogy assuming you had lived those values; think about what people would say about you as they remember and celebrate your life.

- Think about the ways that your life, as you are living it right now, might be out of balance with those values. Use those insights to be kind to yourself and guide you in the week ahead.

RITUAL

5

Meditation: An Act of Love

As a culture, we are obsessed with improvement! Thousands of self-help and personal transformation books flood the market. And if we're not careful, this book you are now reading could be seen as another way to fix yourself. Many of us probably started meditation as a way to make ourselves better. We've heard that meditation will strengthen our brains, lower our heart rates, improve our immune system, and make us smarter, more patient, less stressed—and we want that! All of it! So, we sit on our cushion and say, *Okay mindfulness, do your trick!* And maybe the first few times we try it, we do feel calmer and less stressed and think, *Aha! it's working!* But then there are other times that we remain jumpy, agitated, distracted. What's our attitude toward meditation and toward ourselves then?

If you think you need fixing, you're starting with the assumption that something is wrong. Have you ever had friends who take it upon themselves to point out all the things that are wrong with you and then try to fix you? If you have, I don't imagine you love spending time in those relationships. But that's the kind of relationship we often have with ourselves.

What would it be like instead to relax into full acceptance of your humanness—to really use your meditation practice as an act of love for yourself?

 ## Savor the Warmth of Acceptance

Imagine a friend or loved one—a grandparent, a teacher, even a deity or historical person you admire—who you know truly loves you for exactly who you are, warts and all. It could even be your pet looking up at you with unconditional love. Allow the face, the eyes of this being to emerge in your imagination. Rest in the warm gaze of this dear one. How does it feel to be surrounded with this accepting presence? There's no agenda with you, no need for you to "improve" right now. You can be at peace just as you are. See if you can feel the knots of endless self-improvement loosening. Now just rest in this awareness.

When we allow this kind of attention to our experience of ourselves in the moment, meditation becomes an adventure of discovery about the human condition rather than a self-improvement project. And the funny thing is, the less we strive to fix ourselves, the more our unconscious reactivity melts away. We discover that the loving heart we've been longing to find has been right there the whole time. This is meditation as an act of love.

Easing Your Body, Your Mind

As you cultivate ease in your body, your mind will follow.

- This week, when you sit down to practice, bring your attention to your body. Notice any tightness or tension.

- Imagine a warm, open smile shining through your forehead and around your eyes. Let the soft ease of that smile relax your eyes.

- Bring your attention to your jaw and tongue. Let the friendliness and ease of that smile widen and soften your mouth.

- Now become aware of and soften your shoulders. Let your shoulder blades "melt" down your back, softening the chest, opening the heart.

- Imagine your heart cradled and at ease in that smile.

- Move your attention through your body this way until it reaches your toes.

- Notice how this intention to allow ease affects your mind—without any expectations that it should.

- Bring an attitude of ease and peace throughout your body at least three times a day every day this week.

MOVING INTO
THE HEART

RITUAL

6

A Drink of Love

Are you ever in such pain that you feel lost? You've experienced some difficulty—loss, heartbreak, loneliness, failure—and you've processed things with a friend or therapist, tried to change your thinking, recited your mantras and affirmations, gone running, meditated, breathed deeply—but the pain continues. You're desperate for the discomfort to pass. You know intellectually that it will, but now you're stuck in an ache that just *is*. You feel powerless. At these times, the only answer or balm is love, plain and simple. It won't remove the pain, but love offers a soothing, expanded container in which to survive it.

Without a drink of love, we can wither and lose access to our experience of our larger belonging. It's not just human love that we need but also a much less transient love. Sometimes people can quench our thirst for love, but sometimes they cannot. What do we do then?

Fourteenth-century Sufi mystic Hafiz wrote a poem about birds and squirrels recognizing our pain and trying to find calls that will heal it. Can you hear the birds singing? What if you imagined that they were singing just for you and allowed yourself to be loved by the beauty of nature? Savor the sunlight that warms and relaxes you, the sweetness of honey in your tea, a child's smile as she gazes in wonder at a shiny, red apple.

Opening to Love's Presence

What would it be like if you opened your awareness to the thousands of ways love is all around you? What if you paused and framed your experience of the moment that way? Take the beauty and pleasantness and pleasure of a moment one step further and actually tell yourself, *The universe is sending me love messages all the time.* Let that soak into your heart. You are never separate from love.

When I see the world with the lens that captures the reality of love all around me, I feel my heart warm and soften. At the same time, it swells with awe at all of the delight that already surrounds me if I just open my eyes and take it in. When I do this, the pain in my heart is wrapped and swaddled, and I am buoyed for a moment's reprieve in the warmth of simple delight, which I will call love. I drink its medicine and it expands the space in which the pain exists. As this happens, the pain becomes lighter because it's held in an expanded awareness of life, love, and beauty all around.

Quenching Thirst with Love

This week, try different ways of shifting your attention in order to drink in love.

- Be on the lookout for simple delight and beauty, and then frame it in your mind as love from nature or the universe itself.

- Soak it in by letting yourself be touched by the love. Try breathing it in on your in-breath, and as your chest expands, imagine your heart being touched by the "love." Drink it in and quench the longing in your heart.

- Let love hold your heart and be the container in which you place your suffering.

7

Should-ing All Over Ourselves

The mere notion of having permission to "not have to be good" catches most of us off guard. This challenge strikes at our very hearts, because we chronically create roles for ourselves to express our preferred or idealistic identities—who or what we (or others) think we want ourselves to be. But instead of freeing us or connecting us to others and to nature, these identities often imprison because they're not in step with what is actually happening or truly capture the fullness of who we really are. Like an arrow, these words pierce through the facade of expectations that flesh out whatever idea we have about who we "should" be and what we "should" be like.

In ancient cultures, masks were used to illustrate the identity of the archetype being utilized for ceremonies or pageants. The mask served to alert the viewers that this character had certain *fixed* ways of being that we could relate to and maybe even learn from.

These masks were meant to help us identify with one dimension or aspect of a character. But humans are multifaceted and very dimensionally varied, yet we're still wearing masks today. We wear the masks of who we think we should be. We just don't always know we're wearing them. Stop and think for a moment about the masks you wear.

Seeing the Masks We Wear

What masks do you wear to fulfill the roles you've taken on in life? Mine include *meditation teacher,* exuding perpetual calm and even austerity; *therapist,* conveying wisdom, efficiency, and trustworthiness; and *mother,* showing endless patience and nonreactiveness.

One day, I wrote down everything I noticed I was expecting of myself. The countless and stealthy expectations all started with "I should...!" Many expectations only show themselves when things don't go my way or when I don't live up to whatever unrealistic ideals I have about myself.

What are yours?

When we don't live up to who we think we should be, we feel self-conscious shame and think, *Uh oh! Now what will happen?! I'm not okay.* Then we either pull inside ourselves or toughen up our emotional armor or we get snippy and less tolerant of others. We're surely not in a space of curiosity or openness to our own hearts or even to what others might be thinking or feeling.

Expectations block us from being who we are and separate us from the fabric of life that connects us all through our creatureness. Free your tender nature and allow it to love what it loves. To do that, we need to drop both masks and expectations.

 ## Identifying Myths

Uncover your masks and their supporting expectations. Think of the roles you have—partner, parent, worker.

- Choose one role and consider all the idealized versions you have of it.

- Recall a recent situation—difficult but not overwhelming—where you felt deficient, isolated, stressed, or disappointed. Did you have some expectation about yourself—who you were supposed to be or how you were supposed to act?

- Write down the expectations that support that role and mask, especially anything that includes the word "should."

- Remind yourself that expectations are well-conditioned notions, perhaps myths and not *truths* or *injunctions*.

- Notice how your body feels. Are there any areas of tightness or constriction?

- Now pay attention to your breath. Place a hand on your heart and say to yourself, *At this moment, I do not have to be good. I can be just as I am.*

- Allow your breath to nourish you deeply and with every exhalation, let each expectation dissolve in its own time like a soap bubble.

- Return your awareness to your body and feel however you feel.

8

Disarming Our Hearts

What would it be like to live a life where your heart was free of judgment and blame?

Think about this for a moment. Can you imagine your heart being so unhindered? You would live without fixed views that make you believe some people are superior or inferior to others or of how you see yourself. You would be free from the chronic tendency to categorize others and yourself as *right* and *wrong*, depending on your own expectations. You would be liberated from the accumulation of resentments that block the flow of love from your heart.

In order to love, the heart must be unobstructed in this way.

So often we have expectations of how we think others should act or speak or respond. We have a lot of problems when people disagree with us or do things differently from the way we would. It feels so threatening. And it's threatening because we're so identified with being right. And like the expectations we have for ourselves, sometimes these expectations for others are just as stealthy. We don't even know we have them until our expectations are not being met.

What would it be like to let those expectations go? To see others just as they are? To see them with love?

Dissolving the Obstacles to Love

Think of someone or something in your life now where you feel you are blaming or judging. Notice the thoughts that arise within you and how they feel in your body. Don't worry how justified your feelings are. Experience what it feels like to be in the energetic state of blame.

Now think of a person with whom or a situation where you experience unconditional acceptance and understanding—and for which feelings of care and appreciation come easily. Note how this feels in your body. Do you feel the ease, however subtle it may be? Experience what it feels like to be in the energetic state of acceptance.

There is a saying that "Who is it that is unhappy? One who finds fault."

Judgment separates. It hurts.

But be careful not to pathologize judgment. It's very human to judge. Judgment is on the continuum of discernment—the ability to see clearly. The obstacle to love is not the judgment itself, but being attached to it as a "truth" without exploring the needs and feelings underneath.

Bring RAIN to Blame

Psychologist Tara Brach popularized RAIN, which uses mindfulness and compassion to understand experience. Think of someone with whom you experience conflict and allow that conflict to be alive in your body and mind. Then follow RAIN every day this week.

1. **Recognize** what is here, such as blame or judgment. Observe this with compassionate honesty.

2. **Allow** the blame to be as it is. Don't push it away or force it onto someone else.

3. **Investigate** what you experience. Look for tender emotions, thoughts, or needs that drive the blame, such as fear that your needs won't be met, frustration with the person or situation being as it is, or helplessness because you can't change, fix, or control the situation.

4. **Nurture.** Instead of fighting yourself or going into fix-it mode, tenderly accept your humanity and comfort or soothe yourself as you might care for

someone else experiencing difficult emotions or experiences.

When we let the understanding and nurturance of RAIN fall on our blaming, we can pause, reflect, and more clearly understand the conflict.

9

You Are the Love You Seek

This week's invitation is to turn toward your own heart as a dear friend and lover. However, the judgments and resentments we have against ourselves block the flow of love.

We frequently betray our own hearts by judging ourselves harshly. Yet the relationship we have with ourselves is crucial: it's the longest one we'll ever have.

We betray ourselves by

- ignoring our hearts and not allowing ourselves to feel what we feel;

- grasping for relief by running after sex, relationships, substances, technology, entertainment, or shopping to try to soothe the restlessness of being human;

- believing falsehoods about ourselves like "there is something wrong with me that needs to be fixed" and then treating ourselves cruelly until we achieve the perfection that we seek;

- criticizing ourselves rampantly;

- overriding our intuition in favor of "shoulds";

- denying our basic humanity and holding ourselves to unrealistic standards; and

- lying to ourselves and others.

To return to ourselves with love, it's important to warm up the heart and melt the barriers to love with forgiveness. Forgiveness is truly an act of self-love. Through it, we weed out the energies of blame and hurt that poison our hearts and stop us from abiding in open-hearted freedom.

 Self-Forgiveness

Remember a time when you may have harmed someone. Maybe you were harsh, impatient, or broke a commitment or trust. Like all humans, you are imperfect; your actions don't always reflect your highest intentions. Think about the context of that hurt. Not as a way to make excuses, but to understand the context: what thoughts and feelings contributed to the hurt? Now request forgiveness: "Please forgive me for hurting you." Imagine the person receiving this and responding to you in love.

Next, remember a time when you were hurt. Perhaps someone failed you, spoke harshly, or didn't communicate. That person is also imperfect. Offering forgiveness does not say "it's okay," but through forgiveness, you free your own heart from the harmful energies of blame, judgment, and resentment. You might say, "I forgive you because I want my heart to be free of blame, judgment, and resentment."

Now, how have you let *yourself* down by betraying or being harsh with yourself? Remember again that you are imperfect. Understand what gave rise to that scenario. Instead of denying or excusing your actions, you are freeing your heart of caustic blame: "May I forgive myself for harming this heart. May I forgive myself for being human."

 ## Leaning into Forgiveness

This week, practice leaning into forgiveness each morning or evening, whichever is best for you.

- Take a mindful pause with a picture of yourself as a child. Look deeply at this image of yourself at an earlier stage in your life—or just hold an image of yourself as a child in your mind's eye.

- Let this child know that you care about them and that you are here for them.

- Write this child a letter letting them know that there will be times that they will make mistakes. There will be times that they will hurt themselves and others and that you know that they are a beautifully imperfect human and that they are forgiven.

- Place a hand over your heart and feel the presence and warmth of your own touch.

- Say to yourself and to the child, "Forgiven. Forgiven. Forgiven." As you say these words, let it be like planting seeds in your own heart. Perhaps patting your heart with each word as if you were nestling the seed of forgiveness in the soil of your heart.

MARCH

STORMS AND CHANGES

10

Allow the Waves

I once was on a whale-watching boat and the oceanic swells turned my stomach upside down. Years later, when I was pregnant and experienced an extreme version of morning sickness with frequent nausea and vomiting, I felt like I was back on that boat. But the more I resisted the waves of nausea, the sicker I became. If I indulged the fearful, catastrophizing thinking that said *Not again! How long will this last?!* the vomiting would almost always increase. But if I focused on the *direct experience* of the nausea and allowed it, I could surf it. It wasn't that I liked the sensations or even worked to remain calm in the face of them. Instead I just said to myself, *This is what is here right now. Ride the wave. Be the nausea instead of fighting it.*

I once thought that equanimity meant a serene, unmoved peacefulness that rose above difficulty, an elusive state that I rarely experienced. But what if equanimity just means embracing and allowing the messiness of life? Irritation, sadness, and grief—these too are a part of the whole human experience.

Allowing Oneness with the "Ocean"

"Becoming the ocean" is deeply knowing *all* experiences as expressions of nature. Being fully human includes all aspects of life—thoughts, emotions, longings, behaviors—whether they be pleasant, unpleasant, or neutral. We all glow under certain conditions, and get thrashed when conditions are otherwise. This in itself is not a problem; it is the nature of changing life. Opening to that reality, and truly allowing the fullness of the human experience, we no longer expect it to be different, and that is true equanimity.

While white-water rafting once, I learned directly about equanimity and allowing. When the guide, wanting us to experience the water's incredible power, maneuvered us into a "keeper," a vortex strong enough to hold our raft in place, I was knocked from the boat. The vortex sucked me down—I was trapped.

Don't struggle, I remembered. *Lie back, let the river carry you.* You could say I became the river. Finally, drawn into a current running out, the keeper released me and I was carried downstream to safety.

Allowing saved my life that day. My meditation practice continually helps me remember that lesson.

Recall a time when you were in some kind of "surge." What happened when you resisted—complaining, blaming, grasping for an immediate fix? Was it helpful? Or did it just make the experience that much more painful? Have you encountered the grace of letting go into an experience just as it is and riding the waves through the changes?

 ## Becoming the Fullness

This week, we learn to become the fullness of the ocean rather than just the waves.

- Lie down and allow yourself to be held by both the floor or bed and by your own kind attention.

- Experience the courage you have to be with your changing thoughts, emotions, and body sensations. Experience them fully. Place a hand on your heart, say to yourself *This too*, and offer no resistance to what you are experiencing.

- Allow yourself to be fully human amid all of life's winds and waves.

- Like the bottom of the ocean, feel the stillness or gentle undulations of currents despite the wave action—fierce or gentle—above.

- Imagine that your own body sensations, thoughts, and feelings are like the waves. They arise because of the current conditions, and then change. But beneath them are currents of stillness and peace, which are always there for you.

- Rest and feel that stillness that exists along with the waves—and know that it is *all* the ocean.

11

MAR

The Refuge of Now

On the Big Island of Hawaii, there is an historic site called "the place of refuge." It's a place where—whether you were fleeing from the law, persecution, or war—no harm could come to you. In Buddhism, there is an emphasis on the notion of refuge as well. But what does it mean for us today?

While we may not be in need of physical protection from the horrors of tribal warfare, we are frequently in need of a safe harbor from the afflictions of depression, anxiety, grief, or anger. In an effort to understand our lives, we often create "stories" around these emotions. We rehash the past and rehearse for the future in an attempt to make meaning, but often, this just leads to more suffering. When we perceive that we are under threat in some way— whether that's the impact of an angry spouse, financial or health concerns, or mounting stresses at work—the style of thinking that the mind engages in is all about working toward survival and has a reactive urgency to fix things. We can feel tormented by these thoughts and emotions and indeed need a safe haven to rest in.

Safe Haven

So, where can we find refuge?

Shift your awareness from your thinking mind and look and really see what's around you in this *exact* moment. Note three things that you see. Is your physical well-being threatened right now? Usually, the answer is no. If so, know that you are safe—*no saber-toothed tigers here.*

Now, feel whatever holds your body—chair, couch, cushion, floor. Note any sensations of pressure, firmness, or softness. Remember, you are being held and your body is safe. Feel how, in this moment, your body breathes and nourishes every cell with oxygen, providing you with exactly what you need.

Are you distracted with thoughts or memories, plans or worries? Just note that your mind is thinking thoughts. You don't have to do anything about them right now; there's no need to follow them. Just allow the felt sense of the present moment to come back into your awareness.

Being here now, in this body, with this breath, there is no problem. No matter how big our problems are, they are not urgent all of the time—except in our minds. When we take each moment as it actually is, we enter into the refuge of the present moment, which gives us respite and strength to endure.

Finding Refuge in This Moment

Decide that this week, you will take refuge in the present moment several times each day.

- Put some sticky-note reminders in your environment. Every time you see one of these, shift your attention to the soles of your feet touching the ground.

- Connect with the reality that right now, your body is being held and supported by solid things.

- Look around your environment and note three things that you see—observe and remind yourself, *No threats here.*

- Say to yourself, *No saber-toothed tigers here.*

- Take one deep breath and really feel it. Let the breath be an anchor for your attention and a way for you to arrive in the refuge of the present moment.

- Taking each moment as it is, say to yourself, *In this exact moment, I am alright.*

- When overwhelmed by all there is to do, say to yourself, *All I have to do is take one moment at a time.*

12

Sitting in All That Is

A sitting meditation practice is a little like a seagull who sits down on the ocean waves. The gull doesn't just "sit"—she rides the waves and even cuddles into the swells. The gull needs enormous faith to do this. She doesn't really know how big the ocean is, but she sits in it nonetheless.

There is something intuitively sacred and profoundly wise about just *staying* and *sitting* with the enormity of the waves of emotions and distractions in our own lives. The present moment offers the possibility of repose.

But "repose"? We don't tend to sit in the waves. We run. We grasp. We do whatever we can to avoid feeling the unsettling waves of our human emotions—of loneliness, longing, restlessness, disappointment, dissatisfaction, self-doubt—and try instead to make them go away.

I sometimes avoid the unsettling "waves" by surfing social media or the internet to fight off the discomfort of loneliness, the fear about my own deficiencies, the ache of my restlessness. This "works" for a moment as I get sucked in to endlessly searching for something to capture my interest and give me that hit of dopamine that excitement brings, even if the excitement is just cute cat pictures. But then that moment fades and the whisperings of longing return.

Can I—and we—learn instead to stay and sit with ourselves in wisdom and compassion?

Trusting Sitting

"Sitting" both requires and develops *trust*. At first, it might seem that the trust is in a process of calming down so that the intensity of the emotion can dissolve or fade. And sometimes that's true. Staying with an emotion—perceiving it objectively, with a stability of mind—can sometimes take the bite out of it. But that's not the real liberation, because sometimes those swelling emotional waves are huge—and stay huge. They are part of our human experience, and no amount of meditation is going to stop us from being human.

Ultimately, the *trust* in "staying" with our experience is a different kind of dissolution. It is not just the emotion that dissolves; what dissolves is the *delusion* that the things we use to avoid strong feelings will produce anything other than momentary relief.

Of course, seeking momentary relief isn't always terrible. Sometimes we need to avoid in order to stabilize and ground ourselves. But if we don't truly understand the momentariness of the relief, the habit of avoidance grows. We grow more and more powerless—wrapped up in emotions, and in avoiding them.

But when I know what's really happening, I am free. What we are invited to discover is that we can trust in just sitting, just feeling—for even one second longer than we have before. Feeling whatever we feel as a vibratory experience of being human. This experience, as painful as it is sometimes, connects us because it is something we *all* share. We are truly part of a large ocean—an ocean of humanity that longs to connect and not feel separate, to experience pleasure and avoid pain. We all long to be free from suffering. By sitting with it and knowing it as the nature of this infinite moment, we join the fellowship of all humanity.

Resolving to Sit with Compassion

So, what does it mean to stay? What does it mean to sit? It means to

- sit, pause, and compassionately acknowledge what is actually here—in body, mind, and heart;

- inwardly incline toward yourself as if to a dear friend;

- tenderly turn toward the nature of the moment and recognize it for what it is; and

- allow yourself to just feel and be.

13

You Are Here

Have you ever been lost—in a city, in the woods, at the mall? When that happens to me, in those moments of mild to serious panic, I long for one of the big maps that tell me in no uncertain terms "You Are Here." I love the red arrow that usually accompanies the notice so that I don't miss it. When I see that signal for my orientation, I feel a visceral sense of relief. Okay, I know where I am and now I can navigate to where I'm going.

But what about when we are lost and directionless in our own lives? Typically, we skip the orienting "you are here" part and instead jump right into frantic planning. But we can't really skillfully navigate unless we have an honest understanding of where we are.

Even your GPS has to identify your location before it can give you directions. Mindfully answering the internal question *What is actually happening now?* is your own internal GPS locator. You know where you are. And now, you are no longer lost. Wherever you are is simply called *Here*.

Reorientation

When you feel lost, imagine that you could change your experience to simply being "here." You might not want to be here in this moment, but here you are. Pause and be still. Can you look around, listen, feel, and discover where you are? By first pausing, slowing down, and acknowledging the directness of the present moment, you claim a radical honesty and put yourself back in the driver's seat. You may still have overwhelming fear about what comes next, and this may make you feel powerless. But by orienting yourself to the present moment, you have removed the helplessness that can come by not knowing where you are. Reclaim your agency by being here. All you need to do is be where you are, one moment at a time. Take note of the feeling tone of the moment. Is it pleasant, unpleasant, or neutral? Each moment that we experience has a shade of one of these qualities. As you allow the moment with all of its sensory experiences to reveal itself, its tone is evolving. Be at ease. You are always only *Here*.

HERE

This week, practice taking mindful pauses anywhere you happen to be. Use the acronym HERE to frame them:

- *Here:* Pause and say to yourself, *I am here.*

- *Expand* your awareness to take stock of sights, sounds, body sensations, thoughts, and emotions.

- *Reconnect* with yourself and the moment by feeling your connection to the ground through your feet and then placing a hand on your heart.

- *Engage* yourself with a friendly and comforting attitude and take a deep breath.

LOSS AND BIRTH

14

The Duality of Joy and Grief

APR

One of my favorite Pixar movies is *Inside Out*. It's a narrative representation of the human mind, and the central characters are a few core human emotions—Joy, Sadness, Fear, Anger, and Disgust. We learn about how they function inside the mind of a twelve-year-old girl. Two of the main characters, Joy and Sadness, seem like ill-matched roommates. They are housed within the same mind and need to figure out a way to work together. Luckily, they do and in so doing, they learn a great deal about the benefits that each brings to the richness of life.

Joy and grief, pain and pleasure: just as we know light because of dark, we only know one because of the other. We are guaranteed to experience each of these in the course of our lives and many in the course of one day. Our tendency is to strive for one and push away the other. But what if we too could allow them to harmoniously coexist?

 **Integration**

In this very moment, these polar-opposite expressions of our humanness do coexist. Try tuning in to your own body. Are there any areas of pressure, tightness, achiness, itchiness, or other kinds of mild-to-challenging discomfort? Usually we only have to sit still for a few moments for something of this nature to arise and make us want to move or shift to regain the elusive experience of being in a body without any unpleasantness. It may even be significant pain that is here right now. Whatever the degree of the discomfort, just acknowledge its presence as if you are compassionately attending to a dear friend who is in pain. Now, shift your attention to another place in your body where things feel just fine. Places I like to go for this are an earlobe, the skin on the back of my calf, or the inside of a forearm. But any place will do. There might be many places in the body that feel just fine right at this very moment, and these too—like the places of discomfort—are housed within you.

Find one area of discomfort and one area of pleasant or neutral sensation and try to hold them both in your mind at the same time. For many, doing this makes the "pain" less painful and more bearable because it is not alone in the body. It is being experienced as just one part of a larger, more varied whole.

Our pain or sadness can actually be an opportunity for us to open to reservoirs of joy and comfort that we have coexisting within us. Rather than our reactive bouncing between the poles of pain and pleasure, joy and sadness, our task is to become the expansive house of integration.

 Open to All

- It takes practice to learn how to let seeming opposites coexist within us. Try this practice to learn more about what is within you whenever you experience physical or emotional discomfort. When you experience a moment of discomfort, physical or emotional, first gently turn toward how it feels in the body.

- Take note of the kind of physical sensations you experience rather than just identifying the overall experience as "pain," "sadness," or some other word. See if you can describe what it actually feels like—tight, achy, pressure, and so on.

- Now, expand your awareness of your body to other neutral or pleasant sensations that are part of the present moment.

- Remind yourself that these too are alive within you.

- Allow both to be held in your awareness simultaneously.

15

Sitting Here in Limbo

Have you ever been in limbo—in that liminal space where something has just finished but something else has not yet begun? Perhaps a relationship, a job, even a favorite Netflix series has ended. When this happens, we feel unmoored and cast out to sea. Our boat is on its way somewhere, but the destination feels distant and we can't quite see it.

None of us really likes the great unknown! In fact, simply admitting we *don't know* makes us feel anxious. That's not personal. Our minds are conditioned to fill in the blanks with all sorts of ideas, stories, and assumptions when we face uncertainties, either intense or mundane.

However, have you noticed that the mind doesn't usually come up with all sorts of *amazing* possible—and positive—scenarios? Nope. Ever the lover of drama, the mind usually prefers to fashion the worst outcomes—especially if we're already anxious or challenged in some way. Our current mood, whatever it is, will influence the way in which we perceive, experience, and think about what happens next. And have you ever noticed that these future catastrophes rarely happen? But when we are depleted in some way, we will alter the trajectory of the story we tell ourselves in a negative way. And we are much more vulnerable then to believing our thoughts.

Go Beyond

The Indian saint Sri Nisargadatta Maharaj gives us this instruction for these "in-between" spaces: "Whatever you come across, go beyond." I believe he is inviting us not to take all our assumptions and stories about the future at face value. We need to see beyond the conditioned activity of the mind in the face of the unknown. We can go beyond the stories we tell ourselves and see a larger picture, which will ground us.

Can you notice the difference between how you perceive the bare facts of the situation and how you perceive that same situation when you add your interpretations of it? The next time you encounter an ambiguous moment—for instance, when you hear a tonal shift in the voice of someone you care about—watch your mind and see what it is telling you. What conclusions is it making up about why that person changed their tone of voice?

Understanding How We Build Stories

This week, begin to notice how your mind "adds on" extra narratives and conclusions about what is actually happening.

- Before you share your thoughts, beliefs, or assumptions about a situation, preface your statement with "The story I'm telling myself is…" This will help you become aware that a story is being told and that underneath the story is a moment of "not knowing."

- Use the mantra "thoughts are not facts" to remind yourself that just because you think something doesn't automatically mean it is true.

16

Breathing In, Breathing Out

APR

Did you ever stop and consider that the breath you are breathing is actually an exchange?

Everything is in a process of exchange—of coming and going—and this body of ours is just the permeable envelope through which these exchanges occur.

When we breathe in, we experience an expanding and filling from the chest to the abdomen, and even into the back. If we pay attention, we can also experience a kind of tickling in the nostrils as the air rushes past and enters the body. And as you breathe out, the reverse happens. The breath is released as the chest cavity gets a bit smaller, which causes the lungs to deflate and the breath to move back out of the nose.

It can be incredible to remember that this one breath, the one that is happening right now, contains oxygen that has been created in cooperation with the trees as well as other gases that are part of our atmosphere. We draw in a breath and the body goes to work absorbing the oxygen into the bloodstream so that it can nourish all of the cells of our bodies. When we breathe out, carbon dioxide is offered back into the atmosphere. It is then picked up by the trees, because carbon dioxide is what they need in order to create oxygen. Each breath is a direct experience of our interconnectedness—and not just interconnectedness with the trees but with all living breathing things. There is no such thing as *my* breath. But it is *the* breath that takes its turn uniting and intermingling with all life.

The breath is a friend—and also a teacher. It always teaches us how we can receive and also how to let go. It is here, and then it is gone—just like everything else we can experience in a moment. By paying attention to the breath in this way, we also gain skill at paying attention to other body sensations, to sounds, and even to thoughts. Just like the breath, they are all impermanent. We can no more own a sound than we can a breath or even a thought. They are not mine, but are simply the phenomena making up what we call this moment.

Breath and Mind

Take a moment to notice that the breath and the thinking mind are intimately linked. The breath is linked to how active the mind can be, as well as to the autonomic nervous system that regulates both the fight-or-flight response and the relaxation response. When the breath is relaxed, even, and steady, the mind tends to follow. When we are stressed and the fight-or-flight response is active, the breath tends to be rapid and shallow. If we continue breathing rapidly, the body still thinks it's under threat and will keep the fight-or-flight system going. In contrast, notice what happens when you start to take some deep breaths. The stress response system begins to subside and turn itself down. The breath can act like a dial, either turning up the volume of the stress response when it is rapid and shallow or turning it down when it is slow and steady.

You don't even have to consciously slow down the breath. Simply bringing a kind and curious attention to it tends to slow it down and allow it to regulate all on its own. So, pay close attention to what actually happens as you breathe. Taste the breath, savor it, feel its rhythmic flow happening in and through you. Then, see what happens when you move your attention to sounds and then to thoughts. See if you can observe these other sensory experiences with the same kind and curious attention.

 Awareness of Breath

This week, notice the activity of your breath and the activity of your mind.

- Be aware of what you are taking in—through your breath and in your body, mind, and emotions. What we take in becomes a part of us and then is offered back out. What we take in is what we digest and then release.

- When you breathe in, try to connect that process with some intention for your well-being. For instance, imagine placing the wish for ease or safety or love right on your in-breath. Let your body soak it in and be nourished by it.

- Then, as you breathe out, imagine that same wish flowing out of you and being offered to someone you care about or to the person walking near you, because it's likely that they have the same need for ease and peace as you do.

- Feel how your breath connects you with nature itself as you exchange oxygen and carbon dioxide, which both you and nature need to thrive and survive.

17

Harmony with Nature's Rhythms

APR

Patience has never been my strong suit. During periods of difficulty where patience was needed to endure a transition, my best friend and I usually quoted to each other a famous line from the movie *The Princess Bride:* "I hate wait." And it was true. Waiting can feel so prickly and agitating.

What I have found, though, is that things in life operate under natural laws in spite of whether I feel patient or not. Take a vegetable seed. No amount of pushing, begging, nagging, or striving can make it grow any faster than nature allows. And often, when we succumb to our impatience and force something to happen ahead of its time, we experience dire consequences. Children are frequently exposed to the science lessons of metamorphosis by watching butterflies hatch out of their cocoons. And it can be beautiful and painful to watch the tiny, weak, wet-winged creature struggle to free itself. But if we try to help, if we hurry it and don't let it struggle, it will die. Its wings need the natural rhythms of time to unfurl, strengthen, and stretch out so they can be dried in the sun. The human witness who, too used to operating on clock time, forces it to move too quickly will extinguish its life.

What Is Unfolding?

What in your life today needs to unfurl and stretch out in accordance with the rhythms of nature? Do you have experiences, situations, or feelings that you are impatient with—that you want to become something different or to bring to some kind of conclusion? And yet, what do you—and we—miss when we rush impatiently on our way to somewhere else?

Consider this: patience is the persistent application of loving-kindness, or the willingness to lovingly and attentively bear witness to the unfolding of something that is in a process of its own.

As a parent, I frequently need to assist my child in practicing patience. It is up to me at times to be the holder of the wisdom that not all things are good for us if we get them right when we want them. Can you be a good parent to yourself and offer yourself that wisdom and loving attention even when the wanting is strong?

Applying Patience

Look for times this week when you can apply patience in the form of lovingkindness.

- Think about how you might communicate with a dear friend or beloved child going through a difficult time. What tone of voice or kind of language would you use to convey your love, understanding, and care?

- Now, sit down and write a letter to yourself using that same voice to convey your understanding as well as your wisdom about how hard it is to wait— and yet how necessary that can sometimes be.

- Remind yourself that there are other forces at work that may not be operating on your own timetable.

- Remember that you are a part of nature and that nature needs its own time to express itself.

18

This Precious Present

What is a moment? How many moments make up a day...a lifetime? A beautiful video called "Moments," created by Radiolab, explores this very issue. It's a montage of hundreds of everyday moments strung together in a creative way with a moving soundtrack. There is nothing really grandiose, nothing out of the reach of any ordinary human life—just moments of living: opening a stick of gum, waiting for a bus on a rainy day, ballooning a sheet over the bed and watching it drift into place, the clink of glasses at a celebratory dinner. These seemingly mundane and exquisitely simple experiences are the moments that, woven together like a tapestry, make up a life. This short video consistently brings many to tears in its simple beauty.

But we are in a trance that causes us to miss these moments. Life often feels like we're on some boring layover waiting to get to the real destination. It's as if all the moments in between heightened excitement don't really count as real life. We often delude ourselves into thinking that "it will be better when _____ happens." "If only I could get to _____." But there's only one final destination that we are all sure to arrive at someday: death. Why are we rushing so fast to "get somewhere?" And death is only the last place we lose our life. We constantly lose pieces of life when we are not really present in the moment—this very moment.

 ## Missing Moments, Missing Life

What is lost in the busyness of an unembodied life? The moments of simple living are what make up this thing called "life." Take a moment to pause and really investigate: What, right now, are you wishing were happening differently than the moment you are actually in? Is there some notion that life would be a whole lot better or more interesting if _____ were happening right now? And if that's not it, what is getting in your way of being fully present and embodied for *this* moment?

 ## Just Pause

To even have a shot at really living into our moments, we need to remember to pause and be present.

- Use something that can provide a visual reminder—like a yellow sticker or a sticky note. Each time you see that visual cue, pause.

- Let your eyes take in fully what you see around you.

- Let your ears hear the sounds that are present right now.

- Feel the aliveness in your body.

- Take note of your thoughts and emotions, and then gather your attention in on your breath.

- Feel the fullness of this one breath. Let yourself really be right here for the life that is unfolding.

MODES OF NURTURANCE

19

Pleasure

Have you ever been so taken by the reckless and wild beauty of something, and it touched you so deeply, that you felt like your heart might break open with tearful joy? Perhaps it was the look of contentment on your sleeping baby's face, the magnificent beauty of a great mountain, the peony that is just about to burst into full bloom, a trembling string of a violin or vibration of a note on the piano.

Beauty and sense pleasures can be used as a means of connecting with the heart and its healing potential. In *Chicken Soup for the Gardener's Soul,* there's a story of a hospice patient, a Tibetan refugee, who was diagnosed with terminal lymphoma and had traumatic flashbacks when he received his first dose of chemotherapy. These flashbacks caused him to become angry and aggressive and unable to receive treatment. When asked about this by his nurse, he responded that he would rather die than live with the hatred he felt in his heart. The torture that he had previously experienced and the subsequent flashbacks to it had caused him to feel cut off from hope and love. The nurse then asked him what a Tibetan remedy would be for someone who was suffering in this way. Instead of talking about his experiences, he said that he needed to sit and drink tea with her in a place that was downwind from the spring flowers so he could be "dusted with the pollen from the new blossoms that float on the spring breezes." The story continues about how being touched by beauty and pleasure enabled profound healing for him.

Beauty and pleasure soften the heart and the nervous system. They enable us to feel joy, love, and safety, which help our inner agitations to calm down, if just for a moment. Our ability to embrace the beauty coming in through our senses creates internal sensations that are deeply enriching. But don't confuse the beauty and sense pleasure as an end in themselves. They merely open a portal to the otherwise closed heart. Beauty and pleasure are necessary doorways into the freedom and nourishment of expansive love.

Being Instead of Doing

What gets in your way of being touched by beauty and simple pleasures in your life? More often than not, we miss seeing beauty and feeling pleasure because our minds are otherwise occupied with "doing." It's not an issue of a lack of pleasure in our everyday life but rather an issue of remembering to incline our attention that way.

Sources of Pleasure

This week, become aware of being on autopilot throughout each day.

- Put yourself on pause and notice what your mind or attention is plugged into.

- Throughout the day, pay extra notice to everything that contributes to the experience of pleasure.

- At the end of the day, write down the sources of pleasure.

- Note the thoughts and body sensations that accompany an embodied experience of pleasure.

- Use this list as a resource through which you can access pleasures that will nurture you throughout your day when things are stressful.

Mastery

When things are stressful and we're not accomplishing what we hope to, we can experience negative beliefs about ourselves that create a sense of powerlessness or fears about our inability to influence our situation. These can really tip us over the edge. "But what can I do?" we cry. This perceived loss of control over our lives skyrockets the stress and increases our anxiety. Our sense of helplessness around feeling incompetent or unproductive in one area can even be generalized to other areas of our lives, and we can end up feeling totally paralyzed. We're no longer in the present moment and we have lost perspective on what we are capable of.

While it may be true that there is nothing we can concretely do right now to change the final outcome of some of our major stressors, we can reclaim our sense of mastery in our lives in myriad small ways in the tasks of daily living—one small step at a time. By reclaiming our ability to take care of things and influence the flow of our lives, we nurture an internal reminder of our competency and lessen the likelihood that we will succumb to being overwhelmed.

Taking Action Where We Can

Imagine sitting down, feeling the chair beneath you, taking a deep breath, and making a list of all the tasks you can accomplish today: the phone call to the dentist you need to make; the clean, folded laundry that needs to be put away; the postcard you promised to send to your niece. Now imagine yourself crossing those finished tasks off your list. Feel the sense of accomplishment that this creates, no matter how small or meaningless the task seems. This small experience of "Ahh...I did it" is proof of your own ability to accomplish things. You can acknowledge and nourish a sense of mastery in your own life, and when you acknowledge it in the present moment, you are imprinting the factual evidence of your own ability to address things. That is developing a sense of "agency" and may even cause you to reappraise your negative belief about yourself as someone who "can't." It's like clearing away the excess static or noise that comes up in your beliefs about yourself and your ability to accomplish things. This can then be applied to the other major stressors in your life.

You don't need to do everything all at once. If the task of paying bills, for example, overwhelms you, try taking just a small step: perhaps, you could just put all the bills in one place to start with. By breaking tasks down into bite-size chunks, you nurture new beliefs about yourself and your sense of mastery over time.

One Step at a Time

This week, make a commitment to take one step at a time: break tasks down into small, manageable bits. Then, mindfully, do only one task at a time.

- Write out the task and then make a sublist of all the steps needed to accomplish it.

- Once one small step from your sublist is finished, cross it off and feel the accomplishment. Now complete each step on your sublist.

- Stay present with the feeling of one small task being complete and remind yourself that you are capable of influencing the outcome of your life even in small ways.

- Congratulate yourself for taking these steps to remind yourself of your competency during times of stress and let yourself be nurtured by this reminder.

21

Connection

Thanks to our pioneering ancestors, we in the West strive for rugged individualism. But it's a myth that anything actually functions or is even created independently. Instead of fighting against our very nature, which is wired for connection, we can learn how to capitalize on it.

Connection is a vital ingredient in the human condition. In fact, it's one of the main shapers of what makes me who I am—and you too.

This theory has been articulated by Dan Siegel and is called interpersonal neurobiology. Our minds are constantly rewiring themselves in relationships, and our neural architecture is shaped by connection. No way around it. Our earliest experiences in relationship create not only the template for our future relationships but also the very structures in our brain. And throughout our lives, our most intimate relationships—from our primary caregivers and intimate romantic partners to our interactions with our pets— continue to shape our brains. New relationships or old, we are who we are because of our connections.

Systems theory, an interdisciplinary framework focusing, among other things, on wholeness and relationship, offers the model of *entrainment*, in which the dominant vibration of one thing will determine the frequency of something close to it. If you strike one tuning fork and then hold another next to it, it will ring out the same tone. Think about walking into a space where there is a communal charge of fear or aggression—like a struck tuning fork, it will impact each individual who comes into it. When we get out of balance with stress and anxiety, we need ways to reregulate. Self-regulation is really important, but even more important is *coregulation*, in which states of balance come about through connection with others; these are essential for our well-being.

When connection is disrupted, we can experience isolation, which triggers our threat receptors and leads to increased stress and fear. However, when we feel connection and belonging, we experience soothing and security and are nourished by it. We feel seen, understood, and, most of all, not alone. "I feel you, man!" means we are together in this, and that lessens the likelihood of the "threat" that comes from feeling isolated.

Connections: Who and What?

Take a moment and sense who you are when you truly see another with love and friendliness. Now sense who you are and how you feel when you are on the receiving end of someone else's love and friendliness. Really seeing and accepting who another is creates belonging, and to be in the presence of someone offering this to us seeps deeply into the heart. When we only see another for whom we want them to be instead of who they are, we sever belonging. This is also true when someone else sees us only as they want us to be rather than who we really are.

Now, connection can come in a variety of forms. Human connection is the most obvious, but we can also connect and experience soothing and belonging with animals, nature, our faith or spiritual beliefs, and even with ourselves—that is, by how we are in relationship to ourselves. Reflect on all your own sources of connection. To whom or what do you go when you need to feel you belong?

 ## Capitalizing on Connection

Each day this week, take some time to focus on the connections in your life. Use them to nourish you when you feel distressed.

- Identify your sources of connection and write them down.

- Reflect on what might get in the way of genuinely connecting: Is there a stealthy expectation you have of the other, a way in which you want the other person to be different from how they are?

- List the ways you enjoy connecting with your sources—talking, playing, just being in each other's presence, making music.

- Be on the lookout for spontaneous moments of connection and really soak them in when they happen.

- When you are in an experience of connection, be fully present to it, using all your senses: What sensations arise in your body? What emotions are evoked?

- Use these present-moment sensory experiences as anchors for the wandering mind.

22

The Survival of the Nourished

For the last few rituals, we have focused on different aspects of how we are nourished as human beings—pleasure, mastery, and connection. This is no small thing. Darwin identified "fitness" as the determinant for survival, but what contributes to that fitness is enrichment through all domains of health. Indeed, nourishment—physical, psychological, emotional, and spiritual—is what actually determines survival. If a newborn is not nourished, it simply doesn't make it. Although as adults, we might be able to tolerate longer periods of hardship than newborns, we will never outgrow our need for nourishment. So, it's worth looking at what (beyond food) we are taking into our bodies, minds, and hearts to cultivate well-being.

Moment by moment, each and every day, we experience a mix of enriching and depleting activities. Some things we do build us up. Other things tear us down. And yet other activities are a combination of the two—we feel enriched by them in some ways and depleted in others. Few individual activities are problems on their own, but burnout or exhaustion comes when the ratio of nourishing to depleting activities in our lives overall is out of balance.

What's the Ratio?

This reflection is inspired by a practice taught in the mindfulness-based cognitive therapy program.

What makes up a day for you? Think about an average day, from the moment you get up until the time you go to bed. Take out a piece of paper and write down, hour by hour, what you do. Then, next to each hour or activity, indicate whether the activity is nourishing or depleting or both. At the end, take a look at the overall balance of these activities. How do you feel now? Are you in the red zone of depletion? How does it feel to have this feedback? If, in reviewing it, you have feelings of defeat, try and expand the lens of your awareness. There may be other options!

Nourishing Balance

If you have a prevalence of depleting activities that puts you in the red zone, go back over the last three rituals and see if you can add to your day small nourishing elements like pleasure, mastery, or connection.

- Use your daily activities list as a form of data feedback.

- If an activity is depleting—like folding laundry, for instance—can you put on some music and add some pleasure to the experience?

- Being proactive about adding in nourishing elements to your life can help tip the balance back into a more workable zone.

REACHING OUT

23

Radical Compassion

This morning at the hospital where I work, I sat with a mother whose newborn has been in the neonatal intensive care unit (NICU) for the last two months and will be there for at least another month. Her small son is dealing with all sorts of pain and invasive medical procedures, and her mama heart was crying, "I just wish I could take on his pain!" What she was feeling was the universal cry of compassion: the way the heart trembles when it regards suffering, stirred by the desire to help alleviate that pain. Now it's true that she can't actually take away her baby's physical pain, but doing nothing leaves her feeling helpless and trauma-tized. She needed to be able to touch into a much larger container in which her love can flow. And so, in addition to learning to take refuge in the immediate present moment and how to settle her own nervous system, I taught her the practice of *tonglen*.

Tonglen is a practice of sending and receiving compassion. But instead of the usual approach of taking in pleasure and pushing out difficulty, that process is reversed. In tonglen practice, we visualize taking in the pain of others with every in-breath—we let ourselves be touched inwardly by their suffering—and then we send out whatever will benefit them on the out-breath. We settle into the automatic flow of inspiration and expiration, and in the process, we become liberated from age-old patterns of shutting out the full spectrum of life from our hearts. In tonglen, we begin to feel love for both ourselves and others; we touch the possibility of the heart being able to be a vehicle through which we take care of ourselves and others.

When we see someone suffering, it often arouses our own fear, anxiety, helplessness, and even anger—and so we look away. What we have forgotten in those moments is that all people, just like ourselves, wish to be free from suffering. And instead of feeling guilty and ashamed of our own tendency toward resistance, we can also remember that all people, just like ourselves, long to be compassionate instead of afraid, to be courageous in the face of suffering instead of shrinking back from it. There's no need to beat ourselves up for that, but instead, recognizing our own resistance can open us to the universal human tendency that is alive within us. We step into our common humanity and can breathe it in and out for all our fellow humans. We enter into a kind of homeopathic relationship to suffering—opening to the "poison" as a method of healing. We allow our own personal suffering to lead us on a road to universal compassion.

This mother and I practiced tonglen in my office. In addition to learning how to use the practice for her baby, she even opened up to the possibility of using it as a way to connect with other parents whose babies are also in the NICU. She had been feeling so isolated and alone, when, in truth, she is a part of a community of parents who are suffering. It's not just "my" pain—it's universal pain.

Inner Alchemy

Imagine that your own heart can become like an alchemical chamber where the energy of suffering can be transformed. Imagine seeing your heart as a universal vessel that has a powerful filter for transformation. We rely not on "my love" but on the universal power of love itself.

Tonglen

This week, practice tonglen each day in order to transform the energy of suffering and to offer compassion to yourself and others.

- Start by grounding and settling yourself into the present moment. Feel the support of whatever is holding you. Feel the flow of the breath. Feel into a state of openness and stillness.

- Next, use your imagination to visualize different textures of the breath. Try breathing in feelings of heaviness, cloudiness, heat, congestion.

- And now, imagine breathing out feelings of freshness—cool, replenishing, and light.

- Breathe in fully, taking in the heavy, sticky breath through all the pores of your body, and imagine it going into the transformative chambers of your heart where it is transmuted into radiant, healthy, positive energy that then flows out with every exhale.

- Let the breath synchronize with your imagination.

- Now bring to mind a difficult situation that is real for you or for someone you care about and, continuing to use the visualization, breathe in the difficulty and then breathe out the healing.

- You can do this for your own difficulties and for the challenges of others.

- Finally, and very importantly, extend the healing energy and breath to all those who may be struggling with the same challenges you are. Remember that all humans experience loss, grief, frustration, and confusion. You are not alone. Let your breath be a part of the universal breath and the universal healing.

24

Freedom from "Othering"

(The word "othering" was inspired by title of a talk given by Tara Brach.)

All humans walk around with an unconscious neural radar that scans for threats. It resides in the oldest part of our brains and has been essential to our evolution. To accomplish this task of self-protection, our brains have a bias against difference, and they see these variances through a lens of suspicion and negativity. This is not our "fault"; it is simply part of the hardware we come with. We see this at work in human interactions when we are suspicious of characteristics that are deemed different from our own—skin color, perceived gender, outward dress, religious practices, language, cultural differences, body size, sexual and political preferences and orientations, and on and on. Biases against certain characteristics exist on many levels, most of which we aren't even aware of. These biases create a shift in our openness to the "other," and we inadvertently acknowledge them as outside of ourselves and separate from our unconscious perceptions of "my group."

Those that I deem as outside of me and mine are easy to dismiss. I may even diminish their humanness, which leaves me— and my heart—unable to perceive them as belonging to what I know to be precious. They are the *other*. And if I am busy or impatient—for instance, as I wait in a long line at the bank—I may no longer even see them as really human but simply as obstacles that keep me from achieving my agenda. We can really become aware of this when we are driving. Do we ever consider that the car that is going too slow or that has just cut us off is being driven by a person who, like us, has dreams and desires for their day and for their whole life?

This "othering"—our turning people into the other—can even happen with the people we are closest to. When we stop being curious and think we know who they are in this moment, we can miss seeing who is really in front of us. Then irritations and conflicts grow into distance and defensiveness. The spouse or partner can then easily become the enemy instead of the beloved with whom you are struggling to find common ground.

What Blocks Our Seeing?

What biases obscure your heart's ability to see humans in their fundamental nature and vulnerability? Pay attention to how your body and mind react or how your body may tighten or shut down a little when you encounter someone with characteristics that feel threatening to your way of being in the world. When you notice this happening, it is likely you have bumped into a bias. Some belief about the strange *other* is likely influencing your ability to see a real person there. Use these insights not to shame yourself, because bias is so ubiquitous, but to begin to explore whether the beliefs that support that bias help or hinder you in feeling your true connection with all of life.

Ponder this: What would it be like to remember that, behind the visible persona of each person you encounter every day, there exists a being who, just like you, has experienced the joys and travails of growing up, has dreams and has experienced losses, has areas of deep fear and insecurity as well as characteristics they feel proud of? These details may not ever be known to you, but they are there in the heart of all humans.

 ## Seeing Others Beyond Bias

This week, bring curiosity to the ways in which biases influence your experience of other human beings

- For a few minutes every day, remind yourself that the people all around you are full of dreams, longings, hopes, struggles, and losses. Try to see them as beings who, in other circumstances, could be close friends if you just knew them.

- With the people in your own life, try really looking into their eyes and consciously reminding yourself of their humanness—their places of joy and sorrow.

25

Expecting, Striving, and Fixing

Marshall Rosenberg, the creator of a mediation approach called "nonviolent communication," postulates that all human behaviors are attempts to meet some universal human need. He skillfully delineates the difference between the *strategies* we use to meet the needs and the needs themselves. Because the needs are universal and fundamental to our well-being, they themselves are not the problem. However, the strategies that we employ to meet those needs are often what get us into trouble. Our tendencies to control ourselves and others stem from some unmet need, such as the need for safety, love, connection, or respect. Instead of being in touch with the need that drives us, we stumble around enacting the same strategies that we've learned and used over and over again, even if they don't really work to meet our needs. And that kind of fixing and controlling blocks us both from feeling at peace in ourselves and from truly loving others.

A friend and colleague of mine used to say that "expectations are suffering under construction." Our unconscious expectations for life and of others in our lives to operate on our terms stem from our innate need to protect ourselves by having our needs met. And every day, the billions of years of species evolution operate within us humans and keep us doing things to ensure our survival. So, that's not really the problem. Instead, the problem is that we don't consciously know what it is we are trying to solve, and that makes us prone to constant efforts to "fix" even the slightest whiff of discomfort. It's a system out of control. A huge amount of energy and internal effort is spent on planning, on worrying, on fixing, conniving, or fabricating—and all this striving can really wear us down.

Instead of asking ourselves, *What is it that I truly need right now?* we turn toward ourselves and think, *There's a problem here and it's either me or that other person. If it's me, then I need to be different, better—I need to fix things! Maybe I need more stimulants and more ways to evolve into a superhuman with endless strength and mastery for accomplishment.* If, however, the problem is you, then I'm likely to let you know either explicitly or subtly that you need to change in order for me to be okay. And so we just try to fix ourselves and others. We are stuck in overcontrolling and we are out of balance.

What about stepping off the crazy train of this endless striving to manipulate each moment into one in which there is no human discomfort? So much of what we try to control—like the normal fluctuations of mood and energy as well as the thoughts, emotions, and behaviors of other people—is outside our realm of influence anyway. Instead, we could focus on nurturing an intimacy with our deeper needs, our own being. We could dip below all these controlling strategies and say to ourselves, *Honey, what is it that you truly need right now?*

Fixer-Upper

Reflect for a moment on how often each day you find yourself with some internal pressure to plan, fix, or figure something out. And how often each day do you abide in the being-ness of life and listen to what human needs are present? If you were to calculate a ratio of how useful those moments of planning and fixing really are, you, like me, would probably discover only a small amount that is actually helpful. The rest is like constantly having a micromanaging parent, personal assistant, or wedding planner who is obsessed with finding imperfections and putting out fires that haven't even started yet. This is exhausting.

Nothing to Fix

Take some time this week to imagine your life without expecting, striving, or fixing. Use this practice to help find your true needs.

- Imagine that there is nothing else you need to do right now, there is nothing to fix. What do you notice? How does it feel?

- Check in with yourself and ask, *What are my needs right now?*

- Pause and quietly listen for the needs to emerge. Let there be spaciousness with the urgency to meet them. See if there are any new strategies that you haven't even tried that would diminish the control of autopilot and the habits of reactivity you have developed over time.

- In the spirit of learning to be at peace with exactly how things are right now, sit in quietness and let go of the constant grumbling and impulses to fix things as well as the sense that you or someone in your life is "not enough." What do you find in its place? Perhaps you could discover that nothing is missing right now and there is no need to fix or control anything. This moment is complete just as it is.

- If there is something that genuinely needs attention, see if you can discover, with mindful awareness, what need drives it.

26

Uncovering the Barriers to Love

There is a beautiful story about a clay Buddha statue that for hundreds of years was located in the temple of Wat Traimit in Bangkok, Thailand. During a relocation of the statue in 1955, it was accidentally damaged and some of the clay was chipped off. Someone noticed a gleam of gold shining through the cracks. With curiosity and great care, the workers removed the cracked clay to reveal what lay beneath. The workers, monks, and villagers discovered that what they had was not a clay Buddha but a solid gold one. Generations earlier, the statue had been covered with clay to protect it from thieves. But while the layers of clay protected the statue, they also obscured its true beauty and value. Eventually, no one remembered that gold was its true nature.

We, too, can be just like that clay Buddha. At some point in our lives, we experience threat and hurt and so we cover up our vulnerable treasured selves. Over time, the layers of life can make us forget that what lies beneath is of great value.

So often we focus our attention on looking for love, for the gold. But what if we also paid curious and affectionate attention to what blocks or protects us from connecting to life and to love? Because of our life experiences, what barriers have we constructed to an open and radiant heart?

 Allowing the Clay, Knowing Gold

Right now, as you read this, pause for a moment. See if you can muster an affectionate and friendly curiosity about your own being. Perhaps place a hand over your heart in a gesture of presence and care. Now check in with yourself. What is your state of being right now? Do you notice any tension, agitation, lethargy, resistance? Is there any experience of bracing against the moment, or does the body feel soft and open? If you notice some tension, tightness, or agitation, this may be a way in which you are guarding against the present moment. Recognize this as a way in which you are protecting yourself. It's like the clay covering the Buddha. The monks protected the Buddha because they cared deeply about their beloved statue's safety. In your essence, you do the same— you care deeply about the well-being of your own self.

To represent this, take one of your hands and make a light fist. Let this fist represent all the ways you as a creature actively engage in guardianship and protection. Now take your other hand and hold or cradle that fist. Let your holding hand say "Good job. I accept you. I'm holding you and I care."

By recognizing our layers of clay and softening around them, we can honor our own vulnerabilities as human beings. You can even let this softening around the protective layers become a way in which you allow your own body to soften in the present moment.

As you sit with yourself in genuine curiosity, interest, and care, like the monks investigating the layers of clay and what lay beneath, you allow yourself to hold your experiences of clay protection and you access the part of you that is radiantly loving. By being curious about your protective layers instead of blaming or shaming yourself for them, you can discover what obscures your own golden Buddha self. Through affectionate allowing, you can have the felt experience of being in your own "gold," a space in which you have access to your own love. This precious holding and allowing enables you to care for yourself in whatever state you are in. When you consciously and intentionally soften around your tender clay places, you cultivate an opening to your true essence, and you uncover the radiant nature that is who you are. This radiance is what enables you to reach out and genuinely connect with others who have their own versions of clay layers. It opens you to the true radiance that is the essence of all the people you encounter. This essence is inviting and curious. It is playful and loving. It is who we are.

Resting in Gold

With great care and affectionate interest, take note of the physical, mental, and emotional cues that indicate you may be guarding or bracing against the present moment: lethargy, agitation, tension, resistance, or zoning out are some examples.

- Use the instructions of lovingly holding your fist to represent your knowledge of the protective layers as well as your acceptance and love of yourself.

- Now recall moments in your life when you felt a sense of loving relaxed aliveness—maybe relaxing on vacation or spending time with someone who is very dear to you.

- As you think about these experiences, take note of the physical, mental, and emotional sensations of feeling open and at ease.

- Soften the muscles of the belly and your jaw to let your body know that it is safe to just be as you are.

- Really soak in the felt experience of allowing. This increases your capacity to recognize your precious inner being.

- At least three times a day, pause and check in with yourself to see if you can make contact with any ways in which you are guarding against the present moment. Acknowledge, allow, and let the felt experience of one full, nurturing breath invite you into your loving radiance.

LOVE ALL,
SERVE ALL

27

For the Benefit of All

Sometimes, people misunderstand the purpose of meditation and contemplative practice. This can lead to criticisms that meditation is selfish and a form of navel-gazing. Superficial interpretations focus on the Western idea of *self*-improvement and leave it there. However, nothing could be further from the truth. These ideas are inherently false because they ignore the fundamental nature of how things work. The laws of nature are interdependent. Nothing happens in complete isolation. My well-being, or lack thereof, does not simply impact me. If that were true, we wouldn't have so many therapy appointments exploring the impacts of our earlier experiences with our parents and families!

A profound truth is spoken every time a plane takes off. The flight attendants instruct: "If the cabin pressure drops, air masks will fall from above you. Please put your *own* mask on first before assisting others." If you can't breathe and help yourself, those who may need your help are goners. You don't just practice for you. Your practice affects everyone around you.

When we dedicate ourselves to awakening to an understanding of the human condition and the truth of the way things are by observing our own experience, we are always led to more compassion for all beings. This is the inevitable trajectory of true mindfulness.

Nodes of Connection

All beings—human, animal, insect, bird, fish, tree, fungi, plants—want to be safe. All want to be as healthy as possible. All want to experience ease and well-being. All want to be free of suffering and the causes of suffering. Reflect for a moment on these things and see if you recognize them as true. Now imagine an immeasurable web with nodes of connection. Imagine that each of these nodes is like a sparkling droplet of dew. Each being is one of these droplets and all are connected by this great woven expanse. Imagine the possibility that safety, ease, happiness, peace, and well-being courses through the threads of the web and touches each node. The web includes you and all beings everywhere—known and unknown, near and far. No one is excluded.

When you nurture mindful awareness, you increase the strength of well-being that can flow through this vast web. You are practicing for the benefit of all beings!

Extend It Out

Use these phrases in your meditation practice and throughout your day, along with the imagery from the reflection above:

- May all beings be happy, content, and fulfilled.

- May all beings be healed and whole.

- May all beings have whatever they want and need.

- May all beings be protected from harm and free from fear.

- May all beings be awakened, liberated, and free.

- May there be peace on earth and throughout the entire universe.

28

Speak Truthfully and Helpfully

"Sticks and stones may break my bones, but words can never hurt me." Oh, if only that were true! Have you ever broken a bone or had some injury to the physical body? Did it heal? Now, have you ever been on the receiving end of hurtful words—words said in anger and criticism—and just thinking about them now causes emotional pain?

Words are incredibly powerful, and so many of us are careless with our words. We start speaking before we know what to say. Or we may not even have anything to really say at all, but we ramble on anyway just to fill an uncomfortable silence.

In Buddhism, there is a practice of taking precepts or vows to minimize harm to oneself and others and to set up optimal conditions for liberation. One of the precepts is to "refrain from harmful speech." This is otherwise understood as only speaking what is *truthful* and *helpful*. Both these elements contribute to wise speech. If we only focus on truthful, we may end up saying things that are hurtful to another and aren't really useful—like saying to someone, "Yes, you look really fat in that dress." And telling someone something that we think is helpful—like "I promise to be home at 5:00 as you asked" is not actually a good idea if it's not true and we know we'll really get home at 6:00.

Many of us intuit this notion of right speech and aspire to apply it in our relationship to others. But what I'd like to explore is how often we violate this precept when we talk to *ourselves*.

 ## Tone of Your Inner Dialogue

Have you ever really noticed how you talk to yourself? And yes, you do talk to yourself. We all talk to ourselves, all the time. One of the most fundamental relationships you have is the one you have with yourself. And it's no small thing, because the relationship you have with yourself is the one you will have the longest. How do you want to spend this lifelong relationship? Do you want it to be critical and combative—which for many of us is the default tone of the inner relationship—or do you want it to be truthful and helpful?

One way that we speak untruths to ourselves is in our stories or narratives about the situations happening in our lives. We observe something, and then based on a lot of factors—like beliefs, mood, fatigue level, prior experience, and such—we develop a perception of the situation and then add on all sorts of interpretations. These interpretations can be fraught with untruths. We don't just stop with the narratives about the situation or the players involved, we then add on some story of what it means about us. If someone we want to love us has made another choice or doesn't express the same level of interest, we may tell ourselves stories about what is wrong with them or what is wrong with us. We may even tell ourselves the story that if they don't love us, then maybe we are not lovable at all. Not only is it likely that this is not true, it certainly is also not helpful!

 ## Right Speech

Start each day this week with the commitment to refrain from harmful speech. Commit to speaking what is truthful and helpful. As your practice, try this experiment:

- Bring to mind a dear friend who, at some point, went through something difficult. Think about how you showed support—in your words, tone of voice, and body language. Did you speak what was truthful and helpful?

- Now bring to mind some time in which you struggled in some way. How did you talk to yourself? What was your language, tone of voice, and even your body language like? Did you speak truthfully and helpfully with yourself, or did you include thought biases like catastrophizing, black-and-white thinking, fortune telling (believing you know exactly what will happen in the future), shoulds, and filtering out positives?

- Use this information about how you tend to speak to yourself to help you begin a practice of speaking what is truthful and helpful to yourself (as you would with a friend).

If We Were Trees

A tree begins its life as a tender green shoot that reaches for the light. When the skies fill with storm clouds and it is enshrouded in darkness and pummeled by rain, it must fear the consequences of the storm. What it does in response is to send its roots down deep in to the earth. In fact, the more it grows and expands, the deeper its roots go, finding their way into the core of terra firma. In its full maturity, it stands solid and majestic, offering shade and nourishment to bugs and creatures of all kinds. Eventually, it is brought down. Even in its dying and rotting, it continues to enrich the soil and bring about new life. Even if it is cut down and used for fuel, it is of service by sharing its riches of warmth and light and poetic tendrils of smoke.

What can we learn from the noble tree?

 **What Is It All For?**

We, too, will experience intense storms in our lives. In response, do we, like the tree, send shoots of expansion down into our inner depths to establish a root system that supports us? Do we know that the more we grow, the more we need to be connected to our core so that we are strong and stable? It is this inner richness that enables the most abundant offerings to all the other beings.

And how do we see the purpose of all this growth and expansion? Is it merely for ourselves to be recognized in our accomplishments? Or can we, like the tree, know that everything we are and everything we do is also in the service of all of nature?

In our meditation practice, we can become like this tree. We can call on its qualities and adopt them for our own, reminding ourselves that we need to go deep into our inner resources and nourish our inner root system. We can also gain deeper understanding of our interconnected purpose. We don't just grow for ourselves; we grow and develop in the service of all of nature.

 Becoming the Tree

This week, take some time each day to "live as if you were a tree."

- As you pause, and maybe close your eyes, turn your attention toward the present moment and the experience of your body sitting or standing here.

- Feel the stability of your posture and the inner life that breathes and moves within you.

- Imagine the most majestic tree you know or that you can create in your mind. In your imagination, see the width and solidity of its trunk, the reaching of its branches. Then imagine the vast network of roots that anchor it to the earth and provide an exchange of nutrients and stability with the soil.

- Now, move the image you have in your mind's eye into the felt sense of your body so that sitting here, you become the tree.

- Remind yourself that the storms you encounter in life deepen your roots.

- Actually imagine your roots growing and stretching as deep as possible as you sit and feel your own solidness.

- Now, remind yourself that your inner richness is your most precious asset and is what enables you to nourish all living beings you encounter.

30

The Real Work

If everything in life hums along, and all is smooth sailing, and we know what we are doing and where we are going, then it becomes way too easy to slip into autopilot in our day-to-day lives. We can become conditioned to just doing what we do because it is what we've always done. The challenge here is that we are no longer truly engaged in intimately interacting with the adventure of life. Instead, we are on a conveyor belt of trance.

It's the times when we find ourselves not knowing what to do or where to turn that cause us to stretch, to redirect, and find new paths. Our minds can no longer tumble forward with what is already known, and we are forced to find a new route. The mind is baffled, and now the real work begins. How we experience and respond to this experience can make all the difference in whether we expand or stagnate in this state. It's the difference between a stream that is singing because it flows around all the rocks that cause it to change course and find alternate paths. The rocks themselves catch debris in the water and make it cleaner and more alive. Conversely, a stream that is all dammed up so that it can't flow at all means that it will lose its vitality and nothing will grow in it—not fish or water plants.

Living with uncertainty and insecurity and allowing them to help us develop a clear mind and heart that flows toward love and healing is the real work.

In Zen, there is a practice of meditating on a koan, which is a riddle or parable that forces the mind to suspend its normal way of solving things. It suspends the normal striving for fixing and linear understandings and produces a sacred pause. In that pause, which is the "not knowing," there is a gateway. Koans generally contain elements that are inaccessible through rational understanding. These insights are only available through intuition and a kind of letting go into the process.

The Koans in Your Life

Is there anything happening in your life right now that you are questioning? Maybe you don't know exactly what is best to do or what path is best to take. At times, a careful analysis of a situation will bring clarity and will help guide our path. But at other times, we spend hours ruminating and striving to solve our problem only to find ourselves no closer to a solution. How do you respond when you are baffled? Do you get more anxious or fearful? Do you get indignant and bully your mind into a resolution? Do you freeze and thrash? Or do you let it invite you into a sacred pause where you drop below the usual strategies you use to solve things and just tune into your intuitive heart? It is here that we truly encounter our lives independent of the way we usually operate.

In these times, you could try meditating on a phrase that comes out of the paradox of your own life circumstance, such as "I don't know" or "Who is it that doesn't know?" It doesn't have to make sense to you in a logical sort of way; in fact, it isn't a koan if it does. But it can act like a leaven that you can stir into the dough of your life and let it permeate and touch your mind and heart, inviting it to expand. Let yourself be broken open beyond concepts. Invite in a different way of knowing and let it inspire a new path of growth and understanding.

Working with a Koan

This week, try inviting in the questions in your life. Practice sitting with them as koans.

- Don't try to figure it out. Just gently repeat the phrase or question to yourself and let it invite you into a relationship with it. Like a friendly dog that follows you, it can accompany you.

- Continue showing up for your life and let the koan into it, almost like you were inviting it to play. See if it pops up in unexpected places. You can experiment with it as a word puzzle. If you are playing with a phrase like "I don't know what to do," try repeating the phrase and each time you do, emphasize a different word in it: − "*I* don't..." "I *don't*..." See how it resonates in these different ways. Each part of the koan is all of it.

• Trust what you don't yet know. This is a conundrum that doesn't operate in the same way as something that you use your rational mind to figure out. It is a question for the heart and intuition.

31

Path of the Bodhisattva

What happens when you turn on the news or read through your news feed on social media? It's almost impossible not to be bombarded by the storms—political polarizations, radicalized racism, an intolerance for religious differences, financial injustices, abuses of power, confusion about gender roles, and others—in our communities and in our world. When we face these societal storms, we can feel overwhelmed and seek to find certainty and some solid ground to stand on. We do this so we can have some illusion of control in our lives. Many of us may want to "do something." Many may just feel numb because of the volume of issues. It's very easy for our reptilian brain to take over when we encounter something that puts our hackles up. A surge of fiery intolerance or disgust arises. That limbic fear reaction narrows the lens we use for perceiving the world into categories of us and them. Then we feel like we can know things and be sure about what camp we are in. But this just further polarizes us into beliefs and opinions and creates more separation. The constant pressure to prove ourselves and our beliefs as right can make us feel weak and cut off from a sense of both being able to influence our lives and really belong in our world.

In our desires for change, and even activism, we may be asking incomplete questions. Maybe instead of demanding "What is wrong with them?" and "What do we need to do to fix this?" we could explore and examine these questions: "From what *attitudinal framework* are we encountering these storms? Are we contributing to peace and belonging, or are we inadvertently furthering blame, hatred, and aversion?"

 Being an Awake Activist

In Buddhism, there is a type of practitioner called the bodhisattva, and to be on that path is to hold the belief that "whatever happens is in the service of awakening for all beings." You might ask, "What are we awakening from?" Well, it's the trance of automatically believing every thought the mind pumps out as "true" and being enslaved to our reactions to those thoughts. When we understand what drives both the thoughts and assumptions, we are investigating "wise action," in which we can open ourselves more to wisdom and compassion and bring them into our world.

It's not to say that we shouldn't feel our feelings of outrage and anger in the face of injustice. These are important signals to pay attention to and to help us set boundaries. But can we feel our feelings in a mindful and curious way? If we can, then we can make some space between our stories and assumptions of truth and actually form some intentional actions. This kind of awareness and boundary setting leads to more compassion and a healed world.

Let's take a moment to feel into these various states of mind—at ease, feeling a sense of connection and belonging, and feeling contracted and driven by our reptilian brain.

Start by bringing to mind a time where you felt a sense of wonder. You experienced a feeling aliveness and presence, and maybe there was a sense of goodness and care—for others or for care coming your way. Maybe there were feelings of gratitude, honesty, and simple presence. Take some breaths here.

Now, sense how, even today, you likely got caught up in your reptilian brain and felt reactive, where your limbic brain was dominating. Notice even the slightest twinges of tightness or restriction that arise in the body and in the mind. Try taking some breaths here. You can use your breath like a lifeline between what is above—in your thinking mind—and what is below—in the spaciousness of your heart. Use the breath like a diver's O_2 cable to enable you to enter the deep of your own consciousness. Ask yourself, *What do I need right now? What is actually going on in me when I am caught in hatred and judgment—even in being snarky or sarcastic and belittling?*

In this inquiry, you bring a little light of consciousness into the suffering that is moving through you right now. It is the suffering that all beings experience when there is a threat to their needs. You are not alone in this suffering! As you do this, you are suspending, even for just a moment, the tendency that we all have to perpetuate our suffering onto others. You are arresting the automatic chain of reactivity and pain. You do this for yourself, and like the bodhisattva, for all beings.

Imagine if everyone did this even once out of every three times they got reactive. The entire world would change!

 ## Awakened Relating

(These questions and practices are inspired by a podcast by Tara Brach called "For the Benefit of All Beings: The True Purpose of Awakening.")

Set your intention this week to be in touch with how you relate to yourself and others when there is suffering.

- Practice saying to yourself, in the midst of being mindfully aware of whatever you are experiencing, *May this awakening serve the awakening of all beings.*

- Become aware of yourself in the experience of resistance. Watch your heart when you get tight.

- Remind yourself that when we stay polarized, we don't get down to caring.

- Contemplate these questions: "What is your prayer for this life and for the world?" "What do you most care about?" When an individual, operating in community, is actively engaged in this process and with these questions, then there is nothing that can't be healed.

AUGUST

HARVEST
ABUNDANCE

32

Soak in the Good

"How do you get to Carnegie Hall?" the joke asks. "Practice, practice, practice" is the answer.

We can get good at whatever we practice. On a neurological level, this is true because neurons that fire together wire together. Whatever we do repeatedly develops and grows. This is true whether we are practicing anxiety, self-recrimination, judgment, or depression, or mindfulness, appreciation, or lovingkindness. Neuroscientist Rick Hanson, author of the book *Buddha's Brain,* says we are like Teflon for positive experiences—they slip right past us—and Velcro for negatives ones—they stick! We do this because on some level, it has been evolutionarily advantageous to be on the constant lookout for things that could cause harm. It's not a bad system, but it's one that is a bit out of control.

We can either practice perceiving our lives from a sense of lack, or notice the pleasant, delightful, beneficial things in our lives and experience the ever-present abundance that exists right alongside experiences of unpleasantness and dissatisfaction. It's all about what we choose to emphasize, and therefore what we choose to mentally and experientially practice.

But how do we make a better choice, especially with the human tendency to be biased toward negative experiences? We can start with being more attentive to the presence of delight, beauty, or pleasant experiences that are around and inside us all the time (yes, even on those really tough days). But to take it even further and allow those neurons to wire together, we need to learn to pause and really embody the experience of pleasantness or abundance. In short, we need to soak in the good.

Building Up the Beauty Stores

Children's book author and illustrator Leo Lionni wrote a story about a mouse named Frederick. During the summer, when all the other mice were busy storing up nuts and wheat for the winter, Frederick was busy absorbing the beauty of colors, sights, sounds, and feelings of warmth from the rays of the sun. His fellow mice called him lazy and frivolous. They did not understand that beauty was also necessary to store away for the long winter months. And when winter finally came, and the mice were holed up in the stone fence, they ran through all their food. They then turned to Frederick to offer his harvest gatherings. He spoke to them with an embodied knowledge of beauty, warmth, and delight, and they could actually feel the resources he had gathered and were cheered and warmed by them. It wasn't that winter suddenly disappeared, but by turning their attention to the memory of beauty and delight, the mice were nourished and given a reprieve from the harshness of their conditions.

How about you? How do you value the soaking in of sense delights in each moment? Can you imagine what it would be like to include the reality of beauty and abundance in your experience of life? What would it be like to practice this on a daily basis to balance the mind's tendency toward negativity?

 Absorb and Embody Pleasantness

This week, practice opening your awareness to the presence of positive experiences. Be attentive to beauty, delight, and pleasantness.

- Be on the lookout for pleasant experiences every day. These don't have to be huge. Just small simple delights or pleasures—the scent of a flower, the sight of a smiling face or a lovely vista, the feeling of warm sun on your back.

- When you notice something pleasant, pause and feel the experience in your body.

- Note what body sensations go along with thinking about or noticing this pleasant event.

- Note any emotions that accompany the experience—feelings of contentment, delight, appreciation, or even interest.

- Say to yourself, *Ahh...contentment* feels *like this*. Soak it in and let it be known, felt, and experienced through all your senses.

- Practice this noticing and embodying as often as possible in order to develop a new way of experiencing your life.

33

Adoring Perception

What do you see when you look around you? It doesn't really matter what is there to be seen. What matters is the framework or attitude of your perceiving. A piece of fruit that you hold in your hand can just be seen as something to be consumed. And maybe you don't even really see it at all but just eat it on autopilot. Or maybe it can be known by feeling, experiencing, seeing, and tasting it with an attitude of interest and full presence. And what if you took it a step further and added the attitude of adoring, of delight and appreciation? What if you really looked and considered that this object before you (whatever it is) didn't just arise spontaneously for you to consume, literally or figuratively, but that it had a whole life before it ever got to you? When you interact with it, you interact with a complex richness that becomes a part of you.

Every moment can be a gift that opens the heart. But our hearts must be ready to receive and perceive the world around us. By bringing compassionate curiosity to the seemingly mundane objects of life, we fall in love with the abundance of aliveness that is all around us. Experiencing the phenomena of our lives with appreciation and adoration reveals the richness of life. It's what a good photographer does when capturing a moment on film. They feature something that can be lovingly known. It's not just the object itself, but the way it is being perceived and the attitudes and attention of the perceiver. And filters on a camera lens influence the way something is seen. You are invited to use the filter of *endearment* as you interact with the phenomena of your life.

 ## Savor Senses, Practice Endearment

The next time you sit down to eat, take an intentional pause. Check in with yourself. Are you really seeing and smelling the food that is right in front of you? It may feel a little silly to just gaze at your food with an attitude of endearment, but try it for a moment. What can you actually see? Can you notice when you are no longer really seeing but thinking about the food? Can you let your body feel the anticipation and just explore the sensations of that? Is there a pull to get out your phone and scroll through something while you just shovel in the food? This is not a time to judge yourself but to notice your habitual tendencies with an activity that you do every day. What would it be like if you really decided to savor the taste of one bite—or even to pause and really finish chewing before you took the next bite?

If you need inspiration to do this, remind yourself that this practice in relating to something with an attitude of interest and care helps you to be more present in a fully embodied way when it really counts—like spending time with your kids, making love with your partner, or listening to an elderly parent when they are confused.

 Eating Meditation

Every day this week, commit to eating one snack or the first five minutes of a meal with an attitude of curiosity, adoring, and interest in the sensory experiences that the eating offers.

- Take time to really look at your food: notice the colors, shapes, and contours.

- Take time to really smell your food: what aromas do you sense?

- Notice your body and how it responds to your eating.

- When your mind starts to wander, just notice that and acknowledge that this is "thinking." Then, guide your attention back to your sensory experience.

- When you place the food in your mouth, feel the textures and how they change. Taste the flavors and how they change from moment to moment.

- Remind yourself that this food didn't just spring up spontaneously but that each element had a whole history before it came to be combined into the food before you. And once you eat it, remind yourself that this food is now in the service of your nourishment and is inseparable from what you call "you."

34

Harvest Support

Our minds can feel like they are in a constant free fall, tumbling between stories of the past and of the future. No longer grounded, we fall further and further into a trance of thinking. As we fall, it's hard to feel safe and relaxed. We lose touch with our immediate sources of support, which can trigger tension and uncertainty as to where our minds are taking us.

The mind is like a TV sports commentator who's always got something to say about the game. And while this additional commentary can be interesting, it is really a distraction from the game being played. The thinking mind, that internal sports commentator, rambles on and on, and the more we listen to it, the easier it is to lose touch with what's happening right now—our bodies being supported by gravity, the ground that lies beneath our feet, the chair that we are sitting on.

This lack of connection to the felt sense of the present moment can lead us to feel stressed and overly vigilant.

Held in Safety

Babies are born with an adaptive survival reflex called the Moro reflex that is a physical response to the sudden loss of support or the sensation of falling. Researchers believe that this reflex developed to ensure that the infant can access something to hold on to for support. Even though we outgrow the Moro reflex, we don't outgrow the need to feel connected and safe when the ground shifts beneath us.

Now, bring to mind something that causes you to feel frustrated, irritated, or annoyed. Notice how your mind recalls the situation and then builds on it with additional commentary. Now notice how your body feels. Does it feel tight, jumpy, restless, or something of that sort? From here, shift your attention to the sensations of direct contact between your body and whatever solid surface holds you. Notice the ground beneath your feet. Notice any feelings of pressure, warmth, firmness, or softness where your body touches whatever you sit or rest on. Let your attention be absorbed by these sensations and remind yourself that, in this present moment, you are held and supported. This is a physical reality that you can know and feel. When your mind wants to return to its story of whatever frustrates you, focus on the feelings of contact and support. Now let your body soften and melt a little bit into whatever holds you. You don't have to work too hard to sit or stand where you are. Gravity holds you in place. So, no matter where your mind goes, you can also know that in this moment, the furniture, the ground, the earth itself holds you, cradles you, and keeps you safe.

 Grounding

This practice helps you focus on being grounded, which will keep you from being carried away by your mind.

- Set the intention to directly experience the sensations of holding and support that are present for you through whatever surface is holding your body.

- Throughout your day, bring your attention down into the bottoms of your feet.

- Allow this awareness to be registered as a present-moment reality that is available to you any time you turn your attention there.

35

Harvesting Space

This place is a mess! Do you ever feel that way? Stuff, stuff, and more stuff—most of us in the industrialized world, no matter our socioeconomic status, are constantly surrounded by a plethora of things. Although we may be a follower of Marie Kondo and her method of only holding on to objects that spark joy and getting rid of the rest, we can still experience sensory overload just by going to the grocery store or the mall. When we pay attention to form and matter—the sights, sounds, and things that move around us— we condition ourselves to see the clutter of sense experiences. And this can make us feel like we have no space. We may even feel antsy and agitated or even a little claustrophobic. Especially in times where we are already in a tight squeeze of emotional stress, we can walk around feeling like our minds and emotions are crowded and cluttered with all sorts of thoughts, images, and feelings.

In stressful times like this, we may crave the great outdoors. We may feel we just need to get away from it all! And while this

AUG

may indeed be extremely helpful, it might not always be possible. So, what do we do then?

Although there may be a clutter of material things around us, there are also swaths of expansive space. In fact, according to the study of quantum physics (Sundermier 2016), everything in this vast universe—including you—is almost 99.9999999 percent empty space. So maybe our sense of physical and even emotional clutter is really about where we place our attention and what we use as the lens of our understanding.

 ## The Space Between

Wherever you are right now, see if you can get a tree in your line of sight. If there is no tree to be seen, bring an image of one into your mind. Notice how your attention immediately focuses on the shape of the tree, the limbs, branches, and leaves. We are conditioned to first take in the images of "solid" matter and the form of an object in order to identify what we are seeing. Now, shift the focus of your attention to the spaces between the limbs, branches, and leaves. Let your gaze rest in the spaces *between* things. Consciously acknowledge to yourself that you are perceiving spaciousness. As you do this, see if you can also become aware of the breath that flows within you right now. Its journey in and out of your body illustrates how your own body is in a very dynamic relationship to space. As you look around the room that you are in, pay particular attention to the space between things. Let your breath flow along with this perception and perceive the vast space that is all around and in you at every moment.

 ## Looking for Space

As your practice this week, look for space without and around you.

- Make it a practice to look for the in-between spaces.

- Let your mind perceive the extensive presence of spaciousness in every moment.

- As you pay attention to your breath, consciously be aware of your own direct and dynamic relationship to space at it enters and leaves your body.

BEING A CURIOUS LEARNER

36

Love the Questions Themselves

Do you remember being a young child with endless questions—questions about how the world works and why things were the way they were? If you're like me, some of those questions were answered with "you'll understand when you get older." That was definitely not my favorite answer, but often it was true. No matter how much I may have wanted to understand something, even if I was told the answer, I couldn't fully comprehend it until later.

It's often like learning a foreign language. We can study vocabulary and grammar, but to be fully fluent requires patient and persistent immersion. We need periods of misunderstanding and stumbling until, over time, we live into the fullness of the language. When we begin to feel and understand the context and the emotional nuance, we finally experience the language as second nature.

This is true, too, in learning to live fluently into our own lives.

 **Live into the Answers**

Some questions in our lives can't be immediately answered, as they are foreign to our understanding. Don't fear. Try holding the question itself in your awareness and muster a sense of childlike wonder and curiosity about its mysterious nature. These questions, like fluency with a new language, must ripen with time until they can be fully known and understood.

They might be questions like these:

- What should I do?

- Where should I go?

- Which is the best path to take?

- What is going to happen?

What questions do you have right now that feel just out of reach of your understanding? These questions go beyond the everyday, practical details of life and may, instead, hover in the realm of life's purpose or existential meaning.

The questions themselves act as a platform upon which we can practice growing an inquisitive and open attitude with life. We can abide in a sense of wonder instead of anxiety and dread.

When you marry your life intentions and personal values with a patient love of the questions themselves, you create the conditions to one day live into the answers.

Unsolved Mysteries

Use your practice this week to allow yourself to fall in love with the questions and mysteries in your life. Here are some reminders to help you on that path:

- Remind yourself to have patience with your unsolved questions.

- As the poet Rilke reminds us, try to "fall in love" with the questions and unsolved issues that are in your heart.

- Remind yourself that you have learned other things in life that at one time you didn't understand. It's likely that you will grow to comprehend the answer to these questions too.

Potholes Again and Again

Where I grew up in New England, potholes were a daily part of life. The roads were full of them because of the icy winters and lack of funds to keep up the constant need for repairs. Some could be avoided, others couldn't, and many did a number on my car, and my ego, when I would hit the same ones over and over.

Many experiences in life remind me of those holes—experiences that I keep falling into again and again. They might be familiar spousal spats, struggles with how I handle my workload, eating and exercise issues, or any of the many neurotic tendencies that leave me feeling insecure or stressed.

The first time I find myself in one of these potholes, I may feel shocked and startled. "How did I get here?" I might exclaim. Feeling stuck may lead to feeling helpless or hopeless as I strive to find someone to blame for the predicament. I most likely won't have my wits about me to see clearly how it happened.

The next time I land in the hole, I may have actually even seen it coming but couldn't truly believe I was here again. Or I may have pretended it wasn't really what I thought and so still sought to place blame outside of myself. If I stay in this mindset, I will really strug-gle to find my way—and the suffering is great. It's the lack of awareness that keeps me falling into those holes.

But the next time I'm in that hole, if I'm curious about how I keep landing in it and even take responsibility for the habit it has now become, I may actually learn something. This is a really rich place! When I see clearly what contributes to my repeatedly falling into that hole, I can develop new strategies for navigating this street. I may learn to navigate around it, or I might take a com-pletely different path.

Learning Is a Process

What are the potholes you repeatedly fall into? What patterns in your life do you repeat? Do you judge yourself or someone/some-thing else? What if you accepted that sometimes learning is a process that involves stages of understanding? It doesn't help to stay in the place of judgment, but sometimes, that is one stage of the learning. Try to truly see where you are. Watch the thoughts and beliefs that accompany your experience. If you repeatedly think *Poor me* or *It's all their fault!* then pause. Take a few deep breaths and see if you inadvertently contribute to the repetitive nature of the experience. Maybe it's a lack of boundary setting or a lack of understanding of your own needs. There are many ways that we can contribute to our own suffering that, instead of blaming ourselves, could be seen as empowering understandings that could lead to new choices. Once you have more perspective, and you relate to your experiences with genuine interest and even kindness, imagine what other avenues could be possible!

 Exploring Repetitive Patterns

It's a challenge to explore and change repetitive patterns in our lives. This week's practice will help you gain wisdom about your patterns.

- Identify a repetitive pattern in your life.

- Bring a great deal of compassion to your self-inquiry. Imagine that you are sitting down with a very dear friend and helping your friend look at something for the sake of insight and growth.

- Review the various times that this pattern has occurred and try to identify what styles of thinking accompanied the story you told yourself about the experience.

- See if you can identify what stage of awareness or consciousness you are in with this experience—that is, is this the first, second, third, or twenty-fifth time you've fallen into this pothole? This is not a time to judge yourself. This type of awareness requires copious friendliness as well as genuine curiosity.

- Remind yourself that you are allowed to be a learner who sometimes ends up in potholes and that there is no need to rush the learning process.

38

Radical Self-Honesty

How do we honestly know ourselves? All of ourselves?

When we tune in to our interior life, we usually first discover our grasping and reptilian desires. Those are usually the loudest voices in our heads, focused on me, myself, and I—and on getting what I want and avoiding what I don't want. I am the star of my own show. In order to protect this self, judgment and fear can take center stage, which not only separates us from each other but also from ourselves—from truly seeing *all* of who we are. When we can openly and honestly face all the dimensions of ourselves, without shame and judgment, we are free to be both light and shadow and to embody the full spectrum of human experience. We do this by living freely without fear of the shadow parts of ourselves.

We often deny and avoid our shadow selves. But if we are unconscious of or dodge the parts of ourselves we want to hide, they are more likely to hijack us. This can leave us feeling like we are a small, separate self. Radical and compassionate honesty leads to living more in the fullness of who you are—it enlarges you.

SEP

When we fully accept that to be human is to make mistakes, to have neuroses and addictions, and to be imperfect, instead of wasting our energy by fixating on the separate "me" and hiding our imperfections, we can use that energy to enter into a larger and more humble belonging with all our fellow imperfect human companions. That is the truth of things and it is liberating. Self-honesty about our imperfections leads to greater self-responsibility; it increases our ability to respond to the wounded places in ourselves with compassion and wisdom. This leads us to a better future because we are building our future with sound materials.

 **Human Again!**

Did you know that all humans have conditioned tendencies because of our evolutionary brain development? Let's start with the reptilian part of the brain. What reactions does it govern? Well, how about fear of pain, illness, and failure? Sound familiar? It's the part of us that can lead to incessant planning and worrying, judgment, blame, and aggression. With gentle curiosity, check in with yourself (without adding any judgment) and ask, *How many times today did my mind play through this mode? How often was I driven by the fear of "danger" or the sense that something was too much to handle?* Our reptilian mind operates all the time, even if we don't notice it. Now ask yourself, when you are caught in your reptilian mind, *What is my sense of myself?*

Then there is the mammal part of the brain. This is our reward system. It governs pleasures and wanting more. It needs to win and to consume. The mammal brain is what gets us addicted and attached to having more—more food, sex, shoes, or whatever we deem pleasurable. Ask yourself, *In these last couple of days, how much did this system drive my behavior and thoughts? What is my sense of myself while caught in this mode? How quickly does shame come with it?* But in the spirit of honesty, the more needs that have been unmet in our lives (especially our early lives), the more craving there will be. The craving itself is not the problem; it's our identification with our desires—being attached to believing that attaining our desires will make us happy and complete—that causes suffering.

The next part of the brain is the primate part, which is in charge of seeking attention and approval. It is fixated on creating a *persona* or on people-pleasing in order to secure approval. The greater the unmet needs of our early childhood, the greater the seeking that will drive our current relationships. Ask yourself, *What unconscious behaviors have been driving me in these last few days? Pretending? Lying? Exaggerating? Getting others to depend on me? What is my sense of myself when I'm in this?* Usually this mode gets really jacked up when the self doesn't like itself.

None of this is personal to you! These drives will be part of you throughout your life. The more you can be in a curious and compassionate relationship with them, the less they will unconsciously drive your behaviors.

So, the two ingredients for radical self-honesty are impersonal, genuine curiosity coupled with boatloads of compassion for finding out, once again, that you are human!

 Honest Inquiry

Engage in compassionate inquiry and explore yourself. Ask yourself, *What is here in my heart to be known?*

- Open your heart to the light of the truth. You can even try to identify what part of the brain is driving whatever reaction you may be having—reptilian, mammal, primate?

- Try saying to yourself, *Human again!*

- There's nothing you have to fix. Just rest in compassionate presence—an attentiveness toward what is true right now.

- Remind yourself that all beings who want to wake up from these unconscious patterns are in this process with you. You are not alone!

Learning Is Not Linear

(This reflection is inspired by a teaching in the Mindful Self-Compassion program.)

Have you ever endeavored to grow in something and, after a period of enthusiasm and a little progress, noticed that you were getting bored and thinking, *I should just give this up?* You may have thought that developing mindfulness, self-compassion, and all the things being explored in this book would be different from other learning experiences. But what if your doubt and disillusionment is actually a sign that you are making progress?

Developing the attitudes and practices that support mindfulness and self-compassion is not a linear process. It has stages like anything else. Here are a few:

- striving

- disillusionment

- radical acceptance

We all start with *striving*. We want to feel better, be better! That is our intention and that is striving. And meditation practice focused on mindfulness and self-compassion can, in the beginning, leave us feeling very relaxed and at peace, which makes us feel better. But it's a little like the infatuation stage of a romantic relationship—this is just the beginning!

But, like any relationship, *disillusionment* can quickly follow when we realize that it doesn't always work to get ourselves feeling relaxed and in the zone. This is where we realize that we may have been using meditation as a "trick" to avoid physical or emotional discomfort because it had helped once or twice before. We then try to manipulate our moment-to-moment experience to create a specific outcome, and this ultimately only serves *resistance*. Meditation has become a technique, and all techniques are destined to fail. When we realize we are using mindfulness and self-compassion to manipulate our mental state instead of developing compassionate intimacy with life, we recognize that the practice has been hijacked. And when we don't reach the state we're hoping for, we feel disillusioned. It's not the problem of mindfulness or self-compassion itself but more of a problem of intention.

There is a saying in the Mindful Self-Compassion program that "we don't give ourselves compassion to transcend suffering, but because we *are* suffering." This phase can be really helpful because it shows us where we might be striving and trying to "make" something happen rather than accepting what is happening in the moment.

Once we realize that we are caught in this cycle, we can start to experience *radical acceptance*. This is where compassion is essential. But we no longer throw it at ourselves to make our difficulties go away. Instead, we let our hearts melt into compassion when it encounters pain and difficulty of all kinds. We let go of the struggle and just bring acceptance and kindness to ourselves. That's the point where our mind and body can actually begin to experience peace, because there is no longer a constant inner battle with life.

Every Stage Is Important

So now, reflect on where you might find yourself. Are you in the striving phase where you are determined to "get" something? Or have you become bored or disillusioned and have less interest in being in relationship with the present moment? Wherever you are in the experience of using mindfulness and self-compassion to support you in your life, know that you are in a process. Each stage is important and can teach you something. But realize that these stages don't follow a straight line. You will likely cycle through them again and again at different times.

In the Right Place

Use the awareness of where you are today in your learning process to help you stay the course. Each time you practice mindfulness and self-compassion this week, remind yourself that you are in exactly the right place.

- Using the example of the stages above, try to see where you are in your own experience of learning.

- Remind yourself that wherever you are is a part of the journey. You are in exactly the right place.

Offer yourself some compassionate acceptance along with your awareness.

THE PLACES THAT SCARE YOU

40

Beasts and Dragons in Disguise

Fairy tales and myths from all cultures have stories of a monster or dragon who is really a prince or princess in disguise. In all these stories, the only way to reveal their true nature and liberate them from their dragon visage is for them to be accepted for who they appear to be in their monster form and to be truly loved.

Think about *Beauty and the Beast*. The Beast is really a prince who, because of his unkindness, was cursed to live as a hideous monster. After this, he rages and terrifies everyone he encounters because he fears never being able to return to his previous life. He's caught in self-pity and terror, but behind this is his longing for love. One very courageous woman faces him and learns about his true heart. She sees that underneath his grotesque exterior is a tender being who simply seeks to be known. She begins to truly love him, warts and all, and only this complete acceptance breaks the curse.

What are the dragons or monsters in your life? What in your life, either inside you or around you, do you fear to face? What

OCT

might happen if, just once, you courageously decided to face them with loving curiosity?

 ## What Is Here to Fear

Before reflecting on this, be sure you are in a safe and comfortable place. Look around you and note at least three things that you see. Use your eyes to send a message to your body that you are where you are. Also, pay attention to what solid surfaces hold you right now. Allow your body to be held by whatever you are resting on. Take a few deep breaths.

Once you feel really present in your body, ask yourself, *What, right now, am I afraid to face?* Maybe it's the rage you feel but are afraid of. Maybe it's resentments that have accumulated or shame about overeating—again. We all have "monsters" and untouchables in our lives. Take a moment to allow yours to come to mind. (If, at any time, you feel overwhelmed by feelings, know that you can always come back to your breath and your physical surroundings to ground and support yourself.)

Make contact with this monster and imagine what it would be if it could take on a form. Does it have a color, shape, or personality? Say hello to this image; say to yourself, *Oh, so that's what you look like! I see you. Hello—and welcome.* (Draw a picture of it if you like.)

OCT

Now ask it, "What do you need? What do you truly need?" Then, just listen. Does it need to be heard, understood? Try to engage it in conversation as if you were seeking to understand the needs of a child acting out because of bottled-up feelings and unmet needs. It's likely your monster "acts out" because of some unmet need. Can you see its vulnerability, the longings underneath its exterior ugliness?

Once it tells you, see if you can work together to find a solution. Maybe tell it that you are sorry for not having spent time with it before, but that you are here now, listening. It no longer has to grab for control and act out. Its needs are not a problem, but the strategies it uses to meet them are not healthy for you. Let it know that, together, the two of you can find new and more constructive ways to express its longings and satisfy its needs.

As you face your monster in this way, check in with yourself: how scary does it seem now? Once you contact its longings, can you accept these longings and see them as your own? Can you love them?

 Befriending the Monster

Most likely, you have multiple "monsters." Choose one that you will befriend this week.

- Every day this week, write a compassionate and understanding letter to your monster.

- Spend time getting to know your monster.

- Ask what your monster needs.

- Explore strategies for meeting your monster's needs that may be healthier and less problematic for you.

Medusa's Cave

In the last chapter, we explored facing the monsters of our shadow selves. But if the "monsters" come from traumatic experiences, we need a different approach. Trauma can overwhelm and paralyze us physically and emotionally. Our body is frozen and in pain, and our mind is immobilized. In these instances, we need something different than just mindfully staying present with the experience. David Treleaven, author of *Trauma-Sensitive Mindfulness: Practices for Safe and Transformative Healing* (2018), shares a story that he learned from trauma expert Peter Levine about the monster Medusa and her paralyzing powers. Medusa, the snake-haired Gorgon, has the power to turn anyone to stone if they look *directly* at her. Perseus, the Greek hero, was tasked with defeating her. Knowing his usual battle skills were useless when going into her cave, he needed a different approach. The goddess Athena told him that to slay Medusa, he must deflect her gaze with his shield, which would reflect her. He could then kill her without looking at her. This myth is perfect for understanding and conceptualizing the unique challenges involved in utilizing mindfulness to "face" traumas in our lives and to find healing.

The most important thing when practicing mindfulness skillfully is to stay inside what Dan Siegel (1999) termed "the window of tolerance." This is our ability to stay present and engaged with what is happening in the present moment—whether it be pleasant, unpleasant, or neutral. Think of it like a violinist, tuning his instrument. If the string is too tight, or too loose, it can't be played. So, too, with us when we are deciding whether we are able to learn from and mindfully stay with an experience. There is an optimal learning zone for the human being—a space where we feel open and able to encounter things in our lives. But this middle ground where learning and growth can take place is surrounded by two opposing extremes. At one end, we stay so far away from anything that we avoid both exposure as well as healing and learning. The violin string is too loose, it can't be played. At the other extreme, we dive headlong into challenges and become completely overwhelmed—here the string is too tight and will likely snap if it is played. Either extreme inhibits the learning and healing process.

Nurturing the Window

How can we use mindful and compassionate attention skillfully when we've experienced trauma? First, we need to identify our own "window" where we can explore safely. To do this, we can use the same instructions that are given in the gym or yoga studio for safely stretching our muscles. I like practicing with a hamstring stretch because most people can experience some sensations of tightness in their hamstrings. As you lean into your favorite hamstring stretch, pay attention to when you are staying so far away from the stretch that you don't feel anything at all. Allow yourself to soften into the stretch a little more. Find the place where you can experience the sensations that maybe "hurt so good" but not so far that you are moving into pain. As you stay and soften into your optimal stretch window, you may likely find that the borders of it change as you are easing in.

Just as you can feel the optimal place in your body for stretching, you can find a place where you are truly open and present with strong or difficult emotions. In this window of tolerance, you can engage with challenging emotions from a place of safety. How do you know you're there? You might feel a mix of relaxation and enjoyment, and a sense of excitement at the possibility of growth, even if it feels a bit risky. When we're out of our optimal window, we are more likely to feel apathetic and disconnected if we're in a space of too little stimuli, or agitated and distressed if we're flooded with too much incoming stimulation. To work with trauma, we have to learn to nurture ourselves when we are out of our window of safety and find the ways to allow ourselves to move gently into that place.

Second, take Athena's suggestion and use a "shield" to deflect Medusa's paralyzing visage. The shield is our ability to shift and be flexible with our attention. Without it, we become frozen and fixated only on the traumatic emotion. We need to be able to move our attention and not lock into just one thing. Instead of a single object of meditative attention—such as the breath or the difficulty itself—we can shift our attention to places in our bodies where we can connect with solid surfaces and a sense of safety: our feet against the floor, our buttocks or back against a chair, or our hands resting in our lap. We can also shift our attention to something in the immediate environment. Resting our vision on some solid and safe image draws us away from the pain and trauma and brings us back to the present moment. When we feel in control of where we place our attention, our sense of safety, confidence, and resilience grows.

 Trauma-Informed Practice

This week, whether you work with powerful emotions that come from trauma or not, explore the stretching exercise above to find your optimal window. And use these instructions to help you as you develop a mindful nurturing of yourself during difficult emotions.

- Use the practice of stretching to explore finding your "window." If this continues to be difficult, consider working with a therapist. It is very wise to make use of a skillful trauma therapist to help us find our way. Medusa's cave can be full of gruesome things, and we need help navigating our way back into the safety of the light.

- Practice and emphasize the skillful movement of your attention when you experience even mildly distressing emotional experiences. Don't wait till you get overwhelmed by your emotions, but build this skill repetitively over time.

- Practice grounding your awareness in the physical present moment. Make it a default setting for you.

Imposter Syndrome and FOF

Almost every successful person struggles with periodic "imposter syndrome." You know what it sounds like: "I'm not really as smart, capable, or creative as people think I am, and this ineptitude will eventually come out and I'll be exposed for the fraud I really am." I was exploring this with a friend and colleague of mine, an incredibly successful and brilliant psychologist and neuroscientist, who shared with me that she became afraid when she was awarded a large research grant—that she had worked hard to get—because then she might fail and the investors would find out she was just a fraud. Have you ever felt this? I know I have. It sometimes seems that the more success we achieve, the more our FOF—our fear of failure—creeps in!

What is this fear really? It's the nagging belief that something's wrong with me and that to be successful and even loved I need something more. It's the fear that something is missing. This fear of deficiency and of not being enough leads to the ultimate fear of rejection. With FOF, our minds can nag, *I will fall short and I won't*

OCT

be prepared. We then feel shame and isolation, and the imposter syndrome is in full swing.

By default, our minds constantly cause us to compare ourselves with others. We are programmed to see where we are in the pecking order, and if we register *I'm not enough*, then the default fear is that we will be shamed and separated. We are always rating ourselves. Think about the very structures of social media and counting likes. We're always trying to show how much we know and how special we are.

But where does fear come from? The reptilian brain, in particular, creates the primal fear of the separate self. It says, "If I am not pleasing to you, or you don't think I'm okay or good enough, then my overall worth is in jeopardy." But this is a delusion or trick. And it is the very thing that fear of failure threatens us with. When we are caught in the trick, we are terrified that *if my worth is diminished, then on some level I might die.*

 ## Making Peace with Imperfections

Imagine actually saying these things out loud: "If I fail, you won't like me" or "If I don't do a good enough job, then I am afraid I might die!" It sounds kind of dramatic, doesn't it? But that's how we feel because that's how our bodies react to those kinds of thoughts. The ego fears death and will set off neural alarm bells if a threat activates it. Our neural mechanisms constantly evaluate whether there is a danger to the organism—me. These threat receptors don't distinguish between one's physical or psychological well-being. A threat to my sense of self is registered like an imminent threat to my physical person.

The crazy thing is that, on some level, we all are prone to fear of failure. It's human to have this fear. It's not personal. Once again, just experiencing this fear is something we can count on, something that we all share. What if, when this fear arises, we were to pause and remember that just by experiencing it we are express-ing our common humanity? We all fear being "less than." We all fear failing. We will all fall short sometimes, and we will all fail sometimes. There's no getting around it. Our practice is to make peace with it and not let it rule.

But let's also think for a moment about fundamental worth. Is our worth or our right to be loved and accepted determined by perpetually perfect performance? Would you perceive someone you care about as fundamentally and irredeemably deficient if they let you down? Probably not. So why do we hold ourselves to a different standard, feeling we are an irredeemable, deficient self? What if we could change the speed with which we fuse to this fear and react from it? Take a moment to pause: how much might you be buying into this fear right now? The fear can create feelings that are really strong and that feel very real—but that doesn't make them true.

Real but Not True

Tara Brach teaches us to be curious about our tendency to fuse feelings with facts by acknowledging to ourselves that they are "real, but not true."

- This week, pause every time you notice the experience of fear of failure arising.

- Acknowledge to yourself, *This is FOF!* Or say to yourself, *I'm believing right now that if I fail, I might die.*

- Now check in to how your body feels. Offer your body some comfort and grounding by softening tense places and feeling the nourishment of your breath.

- Then, say to yourself, *This experience is real, but the belief is not true!* Or you could just say, *Real, but not true.*

Facing the Great Mysteries

I have an app on my phone called WeCroak. It's based on the Bhutanese practice of being reminded five times a day that we are going to die. The Buddhists in Bhutan believe that this is a happiness practice, because when we live, knowing that we won't live forever but that each moment is amazing and precious in its impermanence, we can transform the fear of our own mortality.

When we live abiding in wonder and amazement about life as we live it, we will meet death in that same way. It will be just another adventure to go on, another mystery to experience. Like the child in the Pixar movie *Monsters, Inc.* who doesn't know she should be afraid of her scary visitor but instead giggles at the snarling monster and takes it by the hand, we could meet the greatest of the unknowns with that same spirit of curiosity.

We can practice this moment by moment as we greet the zillions of unknowns around every corner. What if you made a commitment to *amazement?* What if you became a lover of the life unfolding before you—and you loved that life till its very end? You

OCT

just might find that innocence and delight carry you lovingly into whatever comes next.

Amazement

When do feel a sense of awe and amazement? How do you feel when your mind and heart are enfolded in awe and amazement? How many things happen every day that you take for granted, but if you stopped and thought about them, you could tap into a sense of amazement? Consider the intricate and amazing feats of plumbing that enable you to turn on your faucet and immediately get water, and even hot water; the visual processes, happening right now in your eyes and brain, that enable you to read these words; the tumbling cartwheels of your preteen. Let yourself be touched by amazement and revel in the myriad mysteries that are available to you in every moment.

The Preciousness of Now

In your practice this week, embrace awe and revel in the preciousness of each moment.

- Take time to pause and really consider all the intricacies that go into the zillions of everyday things you take for granted. Let yourself experience the feeling of awe and amazement.

- Consider the preciousness of our human connections. Vietnamese monk Thich Nhat Hanh suggests that whenever you hug someone, take a moment to silently remind yourself, *You are going to die. I am going to die. And we only have these few precious moments.* Let the fleeting nature of each moment open you to the beauty and awe that it contains.

44

Resistance Is Futile

Here's a formula for suffering: Suffering = Pain x Resistance.

Pain in this formula could be any difficulty: sleeplessness, a child's defiance, a partner's agenda that is different from your own. And resistance is the thoughts and feelings you have when you experience anything that you don't want to be happening. It's the fearful reactivity to something unwanted. Experiencing resistance can include a racing mind, anxiety, grief, hopelessness, helplessness, or perhaps idealistic expectations of what we think "should" be happening.

Working with the mind often means working with resistance and fear. We all naturally resist whatever we perceive as causing us to suffer. And it's important to remember that understanding how you might be resisting is not just another way to blame yourself for the situation you're in. All of us are fundamentally programmed to want things to be different from how they are when we feel pain or discomfort. So of course we experience resistance!

Even though it's totally natural to not be okay with our difficulties, whenever we continually grasp after a different reality than the one we are actually in or actively resist our current experience, we inadvertently increase all the unpleasant effects of fear. These agitated states tell the body that there is some kind of crisis—something to be afraid of. Then, as a way of trying to protect itself, the body goes into fight-or-flight mode. We get ourselves into a loop of suffering that just compounds itself.

 ## Fear: The Root of Resistance

Fear is at the root of resistance. So, let's experiment with turning toward fear itself and getting to know it. We can lean into relating *to* the fear rather than resisting *because of* the fear. Compassionate curiosity is the opposite of resistance.

Here are three questions to help you explore fear and resistance with the help of a friend or trusted person or with your own journal. Try posing each one three times before moving on to the next one, by either having someone ask it of you or using your journal to ask it of yourself. This is an approach used successfully by Nancy Bardacke in her Mindfulness-Based Childbirth and Parenting program. Each time after the question is asked, pause and allow an answer to rise to the surface. And each time after you answer the same question, the asker simply replies, "Thank you." There is no commentary or further investigation.

So, let's try it:

Please tell me one thing you feel in your body when you feel fear? This is about getting out of the head at first and seeing what shows up in the body in response to fear.

Please tell me one thought that causes fear to arise when you think about the future? Here we explore the fact that all fears are *thoughts* about the future.

Now choose one of the fears that you just made known and ask: *Please tell me, should what you fear come to pass, what inner and outer resources do you have to help you cope?* It very well may be that what you fear does happen. Okay, then what? We don't usually get to that place. We usually stay spinning in the terrifying possibilities. But all of us have incredible sources of support, strength, and resilience. Considering your abilities to cope is an incredibly powerful strategy when investigating fear.

Is there anything you can do now to decrease the likelihood of what you fear coming to pass? Maybe there is, and maybe there isn't, but at least you afford yourself the opportunity to be proactive rather than just locked in fearful resistance.

You might not be able to make all fear and resistance go away, but you do not need to be defined by it.

Facing Fear and Resistance

As your practice this week, instead of resisting or running from your fear, engage it and learn from it.

- When you experience fear and resistance, give yourself this message: *If fear is here, I am about to grow.*

- Practice the inquiry exercise we did in the reflection above.

- Gather some friends and together explore fears by anonymously writing them down. Then put them in a basket and take turns reading them to each other. You will discover that it's not *my* fear, it's *the* fear. Fear is a universal experience.

- When we know our connectedness, we can handle the fear.

NOVEMBER

GRATITUDE AND APPRECIATIVE JOY

45

Gratitude: The Happy Heart

It's that time of year again. As the last few months of the calendar year come to a close and the days get shorter, traditions of feasting with loved ones and contemplating gratitude become the norm. In the U.S., it's almost a commercial imperative to "get grateful," including speaking your gratitude (whether you're ready to share or not) around the dinner table. So, what is it about gratitude that's such a big deal?

Robert Emmons, a leading researcher on gratitude, says that gratitude enables us to recognize and affirm goodness in our lives and in the world. Instead of our tendency to stay fused with our negativity bias, even when things are challenging, we are able to acknowledge the ways in which goodness comes into our lives through the gifts we receive. Even if what we are grateful for are our own traits—like creativity, athleticism, or hair thickness—gratitude recognizes the cooperation of others and the benefits of outside sources. Emmons's research shows that gratitude has physical, psychological, and social benefits.

As we all probably know from experience, our emotional selves crave novelty. So, it's easy for good feelings to pass quickly and get swept up in the hustle and bustle of all sorts of emotional stimuli. But gratitude guides us into the present moment and makes us appreciate the value of something. And when there is appreciation, we can actually get more benefit from the experience. Gratitude also has the ability to block out negative emotions like envy, resentment, and regret, which are happiness killers. Experiencing gratitude regularly makes us more stress-hardy and able to feel our own value, because of the belief that sources outside ourselves nourish and benefit our lives.

 ## Cultivating Gratitude

So, instead of waiting until Thanksgiving, you can cultivate this healing mind state on a regular basis. A popular recommendation is to keep a gratitude journal, which many of us have tried with inconsistent results—perhaps because we started doing it by rote. Let's consider how to fully reap the benefits of a gratitude journal.

To start with, it's important to keep connected to the reason why we're doing the journal. And instead of just making a list of one-word things, allow yourself to elaborate. Recall and savor the feelings that arise when you remember this blessing. Research shows that being grateful for people can have even greater benefits than for things. So, bring to mind the ways this person specifically benefits you and brings goodness to your life. Soak it in. Reflect on what life would be like without this person or thing. Recall unexpected or surprising events. Now take out some paper or a journal and write down your reflections. Or share with the person you are grateful for how they have touched your life. By using concrete language, whether in writing or out loud, we deepen the emotional impact of those people and things for which we are grateful, making us even more aware of them.

To keep this practice alive and fully reap its benefits, do it just once per week. This may seem counterintuitive, but it prevents our doing the practice by rote and becoming numb to the positive impact. What really matters is our level of presence and engagement. When you do it, really make it count.

 ## Savor and Relish

Here are some helpful instructions inspired by the work of gratitude researcher Robert Emmons.

- Begin by setting an intention to spend time diving into gratitude at least once a week.

- Make a conscious effort to associate whatever you are grateful for with the word "gift."

- Be aware of your feelings and how you "relish" and "savor" this gift in your imagination.

- Take the time to be especially aware of the depth of your gratitude.

- Try not to hurry through this exercise as if it were just another item on your to-do list. Let your gratitude journaling be really different from merely listing a bunch of pleasant things in your life.

46

Smiling and Laughter as Medicine

We all know how panic, agitation, and distress can directly impact our biological functioning. Well, positive emotions do too. Laughter and smiling work for our own healing and well-being. According to the writer Norman Cousins, well-known for his experience of healing from disease through laughter, the brain is a natural pharmaceutical factory that makes at least thirty-four primary substances. When we feel panic and powerlessness, our brain can't access them as well. But when we experience merriment, playful discovery, and the ability to revel in the sometimes absurd and incongruous situations of life, then all sorts of things are possible.

Want more feel-good neurotransmitters such as dopamine, endorphins, and serotonin bathing your brain? Then laugh and smile more! When you laugh, it feels good, but it also does good for your body. Hearty laughter boosts your heart rate and blood pressure, which is followed by relaxation and lower blood pressure. All that increase in circulation enhances your metabolic and immune functions. Laughter is even proven to improve digestion and reduce muscle tension. All that can result in reduced pain and

NOV

better sleep. No wonder comedians have such a long-standing tradition throughout history!

Even smiling has a positive impact on your brain's neuropeptides, chemicals that regulate almost all cell processes, including their communication with each other. These little guys influence your brain, body, and behavior in many major ways. Basically, they tell your body whether you are happy, sad, angry, or any other emotional state. Putting a smile on your face can trick your body into raising your mood. Those feel-good chemicals can raise your spirits and calm your nervous system.

 ## What Does It for You?

What I find funny may not be at all funny to you. Humor can be difficult to define and is very subjective. Let's consider some of its qualities. Bring to mind something that you have heard, seen, or read that caused you to laugh—good and long. Did it spark something in your mind or thinking? Then it had some wit, the first ingredient. How did it make you feel? Was it joyful, surprising, merry in its absurdity? Now we've got the emotional component of mirth kicking in. And finally, did your body get involved? What did the laughter feel like? What were the aftereffects on your mood? When you were in the middle of the laughter, could your mind attach to negative thoughts?

Now, let the corners of your mouth slightly turn up. Allow the beginnings of a smile to form at the back of your throat. Let your eyes soften as you imagine a broad and loving smile spreading behind them. The feedback from the skeletal muscles used in facial expressions plays a direct role in regulating emotion and behavior. Okay, what if don't think you have anything to smile about? Fake it. Just let your face rest in this posture—a kind of *smile yoga*—and notice the impact that it has on your mood right now.

If you have a sitting meditation practice, smiling with your mouth and eyes can bring an air of relaxed welcome for your breath, body sensations, or thoughts running through your mind. You can practice bringing a smile to your face in this way as you drive your car, sit in a meeting, or listen to your child.

 ## Smiling and Laughing in Action

Throughout this entire week, be conscious about making opportunities to laugh and smile and soak it in as medicine.

- Try taking a humor day: watch your favorite comedies and soak in the health benefits of laughter.

- Practice the smile yoga in your meditation practice and throughout your day.

- Make opportunities for merriment and laughter. Create holidays that are silly and have no purpose other than to laugh and play. For instance, you could celebrate Dr. Seuss's birthday by eating green eggs and ham, reading his books with friends, or watching one of his movies. (Ted Geisel, aka Dr. Seuss, was born on March 2. But who cares? Make any day you want Dr. Seuss Day!)

- Make a commitment to bring humor, laughter, and delight into your life.

NOV

47

Power of Attention

What are we paying attention to?

On social media, when we "like" or pay attention to certain posts, these influence the algorithm used to create our news feed and what we see on the page. And if they're connected to other pages, the data transfers to those other sites as well. Pretty soon, all we see grows out of what we give attention to. One time I lazily opened a post about pet beds. For months, I was fed advertisements about various pet bed companies and articles about pet comfort and health.

This phenomenon is as true in our real life as it is online. What we attend to in our moment-to-moment experiences becomes our truth and the story for our lives. If you suffered some accident or illness, you can either focus on how you have been victimized or on how you have survived, been brave, or triumphed. What we pay attention to becomes the data that shapes our story of our lives and also who we know ourselves to be in the world.

But attention has more power than just data collection. Attention is the mother of both knowledge and love. Without a quality of affectionate interest, bare attention is merely a report.

A Kind and Loving Attention

What is the intention or attitude of the "seeing" behind the attention?

Have you ever received a gaze of acceptance and love so simple that it healed something deep inside you? The pure attention from someone who didn't want anything from you, or didn't need you to be any different than who you are? Someone completely present with you and paying attention to you because they cared? Maybe it was a person—or maybe your dog?

As infants, we require this kind of attention. Our survival depends on it. So often we say of children who are acting up that "they just want some attention." Yes! And because they know they need that attentive connection, they engage in troublesome behaviors to get it.

And what about us now that we are adults? Every relationship—even with yourself—requires investment of time, heart, and attention. This means time to sit with yourself, to inquire and then to listen, to enjoy your own good company with attentive friendship and understanding. That is what you are devoting yourself to. And as you stay present with yourself, you begin to know the fullness of your own mind and your own heart. As you lovingly attend to the patterns and habits of the mind, you begin to know its nature and you are liberated from the trance of your own stories. This knowledge creates a portal to freedom, which begins with the direction and quality of your attention.

 ## Paying Attention—to Attention

For your practice this week, become aware of where you place your attention.

- Make a commitment to inquire into yourself: *What am I paying attention to?*

- Ask yourself, *Does what I frequently attend to nourish or deplete me?* If you can focus on something else, see what happens if you do.

- Is there a way in which you pay attention to things in your life that creates a negative or unhelpful fixed view on the situation?

- What are the qualities behind your attention toward yourself and toward others?

48

Loving the Life Within

I had a client once who told me of "a sad empty place" inside her that felt ancient. She felt so weighted by this place in her heart. She wanted to know what was inside and allow it to be healed, but she felt helpless in knowing how to begin attending to it. As she spoke, I had the image that inside the empty place was a kind of wild Sleeping Beauty self, grown over for years with foliage and bracken. She waits for someone to awaken her and listen to the wisdom she has to offer. The prince represents the heroic side of ourselves. He ventures through the overgrowth and reveals the sleeping princess. He then kisses her lips to awaken her.

This wild self is often hidden under the overgrowth and denseness of all our conditioned ways of being. It's obscured behind our longings, aversions, distractions, and doubts. But inside that seemingly hollow space is a vast beingness that is not defined by these things. This "wild self" is a vast field of vibratory aliveness that is always here. In meditation, and self-compassion specifically, that prince's kiss is like the inner touch of our loving attention. The breath, too, can be like a kiss that makes contact with the

NOV

wild and hidden places inside. It is a loving caress that awakens what's there so it can be awakened and known.

Awakening to Aliveness

Take a moment to let your belly soften. Let go of the tendency of the abdomen to tighten as a kind of protective armoring. Just let it be soft, open, and at ease. Now, notice the dense solidity of the body, while perhaps intuiting a vibratory field of aliveness just below the surface.

To test this out, without looking at them, feel that you have hands and rest your attention there. Feel the energetic aliveness of the hands. Now let that aliveness spread throughout your body. Be at ease and breathe in, letting yourself be touched and kissed from the inside by the breath. Let that kiss awaken all that lies dormant, waiting to be known. As you breathe out, feel the softening and releasing that is the other side of the wave of this breath. Feel that, even in the release, there is still an awake and vibratory self. This vibrational field is the infinite vastness of your own alive being.

As you attend to this field—beyond personality, thoughts, beliefs, history, or conditioning—you open to a loving devotion of the life inside. By making contact with ourselves in this way, we build sensitivity to our true selves. This helps free us from our limiting and small stories. Instead, we enter the wild space of the energetics of our beingness and awaken to our true vast nature—aliveness.

 ## Embracing Your Wild Aliveness

This week, set the intention to enter and explore your wild aliveness. Open yourself to being and becoming who you most deeply are.

- Develop a daily habit of connecting with your own wild aliveness. Lovingly be with your own being and make contact with the life inside you.

- Recognize this as your true nature that is beyond all self-doubt, judgments, and fears.

- When you find yourself caught in the small sense of "me"—whether through a tightness in your body or in stories and thoughts the mind is producing—no problem. Just allow yourself to once again expand your awareness and be open to the aliveness that is always there.

DARKNESS AND LIGHT

49

Moving into Darkness

When the caterpillar goes into the darkness of the cocoon, does it believe it is dying or transforming? Is it afraid, or is it resting and cooperating in the mysterious process of change? The caterpillar has to digest itself and allow itself to become a liquid soup. Not a useless blob, but a primordial liquid material full of potential.

Do the trees feel the same way when they lose their leaves in the fall? Or do they know that it is just a necessary stage of rest that will always provide just what's needed for next spring's blossoming?

All of us begin our lives in the darkness of the womb. We grow in that darkness while resting and floating. But sometimes, when periods of darkness hit our lives, we get caught in limiting beliefs and reactive patterns. And instead of evolving and developing, we push against the pressure from the squeeze of the cocoon. This is suffering. The darkness has become a prison instead of a chamber of potential.

So, in times of darkness in our own lives, what would it be like to perceive it as a kind of rebirthing—a time of opening to the mysteries of transformation and resilience? Whether it is the seasonal darkness of winter, or the darkness of difficulty and pain, can we open to the possibility of power and promise?

 ## From Tomb to Womb

During the tumultuous political times that followed the 2016 U.S. election, lawyer and activist Valerie Kaur gave a speech at the Metropolitan Church in Washington, DC, in which she asked the crowd, "What if these times are not the darkness of the tomb, but the darkness of the womb?" She was speaking about the need to change our perspective in order to stand up for our fellow humans who are deprived of rights and are oppressed. She was acknowledging the darkness but offering a new hope. What about you? Can you sense the power in the possibility of seeing *darkness* differently? Does the invitation to consider that there is another perspective allow for a new way of relating to darkness?

Consider where you hold fixed and perhaps limiting views of yourself or others in relation to what causes your experience of pain and darkness. Perhaps these beliefs or thoughts are not 100 percent factual. See if you can sense the tight squeeze, pain, and even confusion that these beliefs and reactions create. And now, imagine that you are wrapped in the warmth and mysterious darkness of the womb. Be still, floating in the supportive waters, and see if you can relate to the darkness with a sense of trust and acceptance. Remind yourself that this darkness invites you to go inward and trust the process. Let thoughts and beliefs be suspended in the darkness of the womb. Invite them to cooperate with you in the evolution of new perspectives that focus on the limitless potential of your own being.

 Womb of Potential

It can be hard to willingly enter the darkness. Challenge yourself this week to experience darkness as a womb of potential.

- Become aware of thoughts and beliefs that pull you into stifling darkness.

- When you notice that this thinking pattern, say to yourself, *From tomb to womb.*

- Invite yourself to use the perspective of darkness as a chamber of possibilities.

50

Festivals of Light

At this time of year, many cultural traditions have festivals that focus on the promise of light—Diwali, Hanukkah, Christmas. Each tradition ritualizes the lighting of fires and candles to signify the light's triumph over darkness. As the winter solstice gets closer and the earth turns away from the sun and the days shorten, humans have always needed reminders of the promise of the return of the light. Can you imagine being an early human or a Neanderthal? It must have been terrifying to see the sun for less time every day. We humans need light to survive. And even outside of the festivals, cozying up around a roaring fire in the darkness of winter brings a kind of holy cheer, a sacred remembering of the importance of light.

But it's more than just the basic survival needs for illumination and warmth that draw us to the light of fires and candles. The next time you find yourself lost in thought while gazing at a fireplace ablaze or even a solitary candle flame, consider this: being mesmerized by fire might have sparked the evolution of the human mind. "Research into cognitive evolution—a field of study that brings together psychology, anthropology, neuroscience, and genetics," reports *Smithsonian* magazine, "suggests that fire's most lasting impact was how our responses to it altered our brains, helping endow us with capabilities such as long-term memory and problem-solving" (Wynn, 2012).

This is one of the topics we have been exploring throughout this book: what conditions enable us to access our deepest, most vast selves? In this darkest part of the year, consider spending time with the aliveness of a flame.

 ## Meditations on Light

Numerous meditation traditions utilize the mesmerizing effects of a flame to support a kind of one-pointed attention. Have you ever had this experience? Remember what it feels like to be absorbed in the flickering light of an active fire. This devoted attentiveness in meditation activates the same brain regions that govern working memory. Maybe our ancient ancestors were good meditators. The ones who most fully developed mindful absorption around the fire got the best health benefits and therefore were more likely to survive and pass on their genes. No wonder we've developed so many festivals that celebrate light! When our ancestors absorbed their attention in reverie around a fire, they were able to make contingency plans and figure out alternative responses to problems rather than just continuously doing the same thing. Sound familiar? Consider this: maybe the most enduring tool that fire ever created was the meditative human mind.

 Light My Fire

This week, let the aliveness of a flame be a focal point for your attention in the present moment. Make it a daily ritual to engage with the power of light.

- If you celebrate one of the winter holidays, pay extra attention to the experience of the light punctuating the darkness. Let yourself be emotionally or spiritually touched by the light.

- Try gazing at a candle flame or fireplace, and let the dancing of the flames to draw in your attention. Let this be a meditation practice.

- Let your eyes be soft and your gaze devoted to seeing the flames' aliveness. Let this mirror a sense of your own internal flame.

- In the evenings, try turning off electric lights and let the glow of candles permeate your space.

- See if you can tune into the sacredness of the flames and connect with the magic of their glow. As you do this, you are connecting with the whole lineage of the human family.

51

Noble Silence

Many meditation retreats are held in what is known in Buddhism as "noble silence." Participants renounce the usual mode of being with others and refrain from speaking. Included in that is a commitment to forgo listening to music or other entertainment and, in many cases, even reading. It's not a punitive silence but one of deep respect for slowing down and retreating from the busyness of our modern lives. It invites the attention to turn inward and to observe and become intimate with the workings of mind, heart, and body. The silence supports a liberated investigation of the human condition, with all its habits and sacredness.

For years, I attended an annual ten-day retreat at the Insight Meditation Society in Barre, Massachusetts, over New Year's. The depths of the New England winter blanketed the retreat center in a profound and magical silence. I felt how much it supported my practice and caused my whole being to enter into a state of deep listening. It was such a contrast to the hectic frenzy of loud, busy everyday life. We've become so unused to quiet. It's even hard for most of us to drive in our cars without the radio or some other form of audible stimuli bombarding us.

Enter In

Have you ever entered a woodland or mountainous place of utter silence—or entered a synagogue or cathedral that was completely quiet? The silence beckons us to pause, to lean into its magic. Awe can fill us, and no words would improve upon the perfection of the silence. So, we just let it hold us and heal us down to our own ancient bones.

It's not to judge talking, listening to music, or being stimulated by sounds. These can all be incredibly wonderful things. But every once in a while, we need to give our nerves a break and enter into noble silence.

Where and when do you make time for the profound and healing power of silence in your life? Can you let yourself "unplug" and be enveloped by the sacredness of silence?

Embracing Silence

Make a commitment to bathe your senses in silence every day— even if only for a minute.

- Turn off your devices or radio while you drive, and just drive.

- When you're out for a walk, walk in silence instead of having your ears full of music or a podcast.

- When spending time with a friend, especially when they need you to listen to them, periodically ask yourself, *Does what I have to say improve upon the silence?*

52

Reflecting Radiance

Although the moon appears to be self-illuminating, it actually glows because it reflects the radiant attention of the sun. Sometimes a full moon can appear so bright that it seems to light up the entire sky. But in truth, the moon only reflects between three and twelve percent of the light that touches it. It doesn't take much of the great brilliance and power of the sun to provide luminous intensity to the moon and to us who in turn are bathed in its light.

Isn't it sometimes like that in our lives? Just a little bit of radiant kindness from someone can light up our whole being. And like the moon, without that touch of illumination, we would just be a hard, dark rock.

But the moon doesn't just soak up the sun's rays so it can shine for itself. Its light is part of a cosmic reciprocal process. Our nights are made navigable because there is a bright orb sharing its light with us.

 **Moon Language**

Why not be like the moon and know that we have the power to both receive and reflect light to others? Every human that you will ever encounter, just like you, longs to know their worthiness for love and seeks a sense of belonging. How about the person who got your coffee this morning? Could that person, in some way through their interaction with you, have been saying, "See me as a lovable, worthwhile human being"? At the heart of all your own interactions with others, you are actually saying that too. You will likely never hear those words in the whisperings of your heart, but they are there in the shadows—just as they are in the shadows of every heart.

The poet Hafiz instructs us to speak a kind of "moon language"—to offer through a light in our eyes the gaze of attentive illumination that every other being longs to receive.

All our contemplations and reflections, practices of mindfulness and self-compassion are designed to clear away the obstructions in our own hearts and minds, allowing us to be radiant and to speak fluently in moon language for the benefit of all beings!

Luminous Connecting

Remember the universal pull in all of us to connect. Let this reminder support you in a conscious practice of connection.

- If it feels appropriate, try looking at the color of someone's eyes as you are talking to them. It's not a stare, but a way to really see them.

- Imagine people in a younger, child version of themselves. See the kid inside that has hopes and fears, playfulness and uncertainties.

- Let your eyes smile as you speak and interact with people.

References

Siegel, Daniel J. 1999. *The Developing Mind: How Relationships and the Brain Interact to Shape Who We Are.* New York: Guilford Press.

Sundermier, Ali. "99.9999999% of Your Body Is Empty Space." September 23, 2016. https://www.sciencealert.com/99-9999999-of-your-body-is-empty-space.

Treleaven, David. 2018. *Trauma-Sensitive Mindfulness: Practices for Safe and Transformative Healing.* New York: W. W. Norton & Company.

Wynn, Thomas. 2012. "Fire Good. Make Human Inspiration Happen." *Smithsonian.* https://www.smithsonianmag.com/science-nature/fire-good-make-human-inspiration-happen-132494650/

Catherine Polan Orzech, MA, LMFT, has taught mindfulness for over two decades. She is a certified mindfulness-based stress reduction (MBSR) and mindful self-compassion (MSC) teacher; and is currently faculty in the departments of psychiatry, and obstetrics and gynecology, at Oregon Health & Science University, where she's involved in research on mindfulness and women's health.

Previously, she served on the faculty at several leading mindfulness institutes, including those at Thomas Jefferson University Hospital in Philadelphia, PA; the University of California, San Francisco; and the University of California, San Diego. Catherine currently lives in Oregon, where she is a marriage and family therapist specializing in mindfulness-based psychotherapy.

MORE BOOKS for the SPIRITUAL SEEKER

ISBN: 978-1684033492 | US $16.95

ISBN: 978-1608820313 | US $16.95

ISBN: 978-1684034314 | US $17.95

ISBN: 978-1684032389 | US $19.95

newharbingerpublications

REVEAL PRESS